ANCIENT

LONG ISLAND EPITAPHS,

FROM THE TOWNS OF

SOUTHOLD, SHELTER ISLAND

AND

EASTHAMPTON,

NEW YORK.

BY EDWARD DOUBLEDAY HARRIS.

CLEARFIELD

BEING A REPRINT FROM THE
NEW ENGLAND HISTORICAL AND GENEALOGICAL
REGISTER,

WITH ADDITIONS.

Originally published
Boston, 1903

Reprinted for
Clearfield Company, Inc. by
Genealogical Publishing Co., Inc.
Baltimore, Maryland
2000, 2002

International Standard Book Number: 0-8063-4996-4

Made in the United States of America

CONTENTS.

---

iv

INTRODUCTION.

DURING the period between the years 1877 and 1890, nearly all of the burial places on Long Island that had been in general and parish use prior to 1800 were visited by the writer, and careful transcripts made by him of such inscriptions as could then be found. In addition to these, various private or family grounds,—those that were most easily accessible,—were also visited for the same purpose. The following pages contain copies of epitaphs found in Southold, Shelter Island and Easthampton, the towns covering the eastern extremity of Long Island and forming part of the county of Suffolk, the place of record of which is Riverhead, in the town of the same name. Inscriptions from the burial places at Mattituck and Cutchogue in the westerly part of Southold, and those of the family ground of the Gardiners on Gardiner's Island, of Easthampton, are not included in this publication.

The larger number of the first settlers of eastern Suffolk were of English birth or extraction, many of them having been for a while established in the southern colonies of the New England States, relations with which, both political and ecclesiastical, were of the most intimate character. In fact, Suffolk county in colonial times was thoroughly New England in its affiliations and interests.

The early grave stones still standing are mostly either of imported slate, or of sand stone brought across the Sound from the Connecticut shore. Those of slate are generally in excellent condition. The material of which these were made was from the quarries of southwestern England and Wales. Their counterparts may be seen in all the older coast towns of New England from Portsmouth to New Haven, and examples are still standing in the old church yards of Trinity and St. Paul's in the City of New York. Their decorated heads and borders, in a great variety of forms, and carefully conventionalized in character, were engraved in the mother country, while the inscriptions were usually cut on this side of the Atlantic. On many of these slate stones the fine scratches made by the workman with the corner of his chisel, to limit the heights of the letters of the inscription, are still plainly discernible; the storms of two hundred years have failed to obliterate them or to make the slightest impression on the original surface. It is far otherwise with the stones from the home quarries of Connecticut. On many of these the inscriptions have suffered, surface disintegration having obliterated all but the deeper cut portions of the letters, while it is not uncommon to find the entire surface scaled away so that all evidences of inscription have vanished. In the light of the lesson of two hundred years it is fair to predict that at the end of this twentieth century but a remnant of the native stones whose epitaphs are preserved in these pages will be standing. The advent of the troubles with the mother country naturally put an end to the importation of the English slates, and they were completely superseded by the brown-stones from the Connecticut valley, which, in turn, gave way in the early part of the nineteenth century to memorials of white marble.

It has been impossible in these pages to accurately represent the styles of lettering in use during the period covered by the epitaphs. No attempt has been made to indicate the logotypes or composite letters which were common on the older stones, and which are, in some cases, of much interest archæologically. The arrangement in lines as found upon the stones has been generally observed, while the use of capitals, italics, and of superior letters has been always carefully followed. Worthy of special notice are a few stones in the old ground of Southold Village, lying horizontally, about six feet in length, portions of whose inscriptions form a border at the edges of the four sides, an extremely unusual feature in this country (see pp. 7, 8 and 10). But two examples of the use of coat armor on original stones occur in any of the grounds under present consideration; both in Shelter Island, and upon the tombs of the Sylvesters and Deerings.

Innumerable family burying grounds were scattered over Long Island, the larger portion of which were on the farms of the early settlers, and in many cases at considerable distances from the villages. Some of these grounds have been for many years unused, some have been ploughed over, and the stones either buried or removed to the nearest public cemetery. In God's acre a fair chance would seem to exist for the protection of a grave stone, but the family burial place, overrun with cattle, and subjected to the yearly encroachments of the plough, offers scant hope for the long preservation of its contents. The frugal farmer finds the flat stone a convenient cover for a trench or for a wall coping. Only lately the Beales were scouring eastern Long Island for their ancestor's head-stone, taken from its place on the farm to be built into a chimney, and later to be used as a door step. And not long since, a search for the death date of another Long Islander traced into Dutchess county, resulted in its discovery on his grave stone which had long made a part of the flagged walk to his granddaughter's door.

The writer gratefully acknowledges the assistance in the preparation of this work for the press which he has received from his friends, Mr. Rufus King and Miss Lucy D. Akerly. Wholly to the latter the reader is indebted for the valuable genealogical notes on the Old Orient epitaphs, and for the Hashamomack inscriptions of the Appendix. While to the unflagging interest and generous help in many ways accorded by Mr. Orville B. Ackerly, in addition to his substantial contribution of abstracts from the New York Surrogates Court, the publication of these pages is largely attributable.

SOUTHOLD.

THE eastern end of Long Island is divided into two long and narrow peninsulas by a body of water some forty miles in length, constituting, itself, a series of connecting bays. The northerly and shorter one of these peninsulas is the township of Southold. It has an average width of hardly three miles, with an extreme length of twenty-two, being almost surrounded by the waters of Long Island Sound and the two bays, Peconic and Gardiner's. The township is traversed longitudinally by two main roads that enter its bounds from its adjoining neighbor on the west, Riverhead, but which merge into one a few miles from the eastern extremity of the town. The first settlement by the whites (who were of English birth) was in 1639–40, though the town records were not begun in the form in which we now have them until 1651. The village of Southold is near the south shore, and at about the middle of the township in the direction of its length. Here was built the first church, and the burying ground, one of the oldest on the Island, was by its side, on the south side of the main street. The inscriptions following, on pages 3–24, are all that were found there in 1884, antedating 1800.

About four miles west of Southold village, on the south road, is the old burying-ground of the settlement of Cutchogue. In 1886 it was in a very neglected condition. It contained then one hundred and thirty-six stones of the eighteenth century, the oldest of which was of 1717. The epitaphs of two of the early pastors are here :—

In Memory of yᵉ Revᵈ Mʳ
THOMAS PAINE late Paſtor
in this Place who lived defir'd
by Many [a diftinguiſhing Preachᵉʳ
of Righteouſneſs & a ſucceſsfull
healer of the Sick] and died
lamented by Moft on yᵉ 15ᵗʰ of
Octʳ 1766 in yᵉ 43ᵈ Year of
his Age.

In Memory of
Mᴿ
TIMOTHY WELLS
Paſtor of a Church
of Chriſt in South Hold
who died Janʳʸ 16ᵗʰ
A.D. 1782 : in the 63ᵈ
Year of his Age.

The surnames represented on the other stones are those of Benjamin, Billard, Booth, Brown, Case, Chittenden, Cleaves, Ely, Goldsmith, Greene, Horton, Hudson, Hull, Landon, Lupton, Mapes, Moore, Osborn, Overton, Pain, Penny, Reeves, Terrcy, Terry, Tuthill, Webb, Wells, Wickham, Wines, Woodhull.

From three to four miles further west is the burying-ground of the village of Mattituck, at the westerly end of the township, adjoining the Presbyterian church, a few rods south of the Mattituck station of the Long Island rail-road. It contained in 1886 one hundred and thirty-eight stones of the eighteenth century, the oldest date being 1723. The surnames found there are those of Aldrich. Barker, Benjamin, Brown, Case, Clark, Cleaves, Conklin (1726), Corwin, Dimon (1725), Gardiner, Goldsmith, Halliock, Havens, Howell, Hubbard, Hudson, Lamb (1729), Mann, Mapes (1732), Moore, Osborn, Overton, Parker (1727), Parshall (1725), Pendleton, Pike, Pritchard, Reeves (1723), Swasey, Terry, Tinker (1728), Turrell, Tusten, Tuthill, Wells, Wickham, Wines and Worth.

East of Southold village, and near the Sound shore, is the little burial place of Hashamomack, the epitaphs from which are to be found on pages 94 and 95.

East of Greenport, a mile and one half, is the " Sterling Cemetery," near the little village of East Marion. The inscriptions here that could be read in 1881, of dates prior to 1800, are printed on pages 25–27.

Still further east, and where the waters of the Sound and Gardiner's Bay have so nearly effected a union that but a very narrow neck of land divides them, are the old burial places of Oyster Pond (page 28) and the later one of Orient Village (page 36).

EPITAPHS OF SOUTHOLD.

SOUTHOLD VILLAGE.

HERE LYES Y⁰ BODY OF WILLIAM
WHITEHAIRE   AGED   44   YEARS
DEPARTED   THIS   LIFE   APRIL
Y⁰   21ˢᵗ   1   7   0   7

how ready he was to help all those that were in distrefs
and tooke delight to feed thee fatherlefs

In Memory of *Mr. Zacheus Goldfmith*, who died Jan. 21ft 1795 in the 85th
year of his age.

In Memory of Mrs. Deborah Goldfmith, wife of Mʳ Zacheus Goldfmith, who
died Novʳ 15 AD. 1787, Aged 73 Years.

HERE   LYES   Y⁰   BODY
OF   NATHAN   REEUE
SON   TO   JOHN   AND
MARTHA   REEUE   AGED
22   YEARS   5   M⁰   & 11
DAYS   DECᴰ   MARCH
Y⁰   1   1   7   2   4

IN MEMORY of
Martha y⁰ Wife of
Mʳ John Reeve
who died May 16ᵗʰ
1762 in the 87ᵗʰ
Year of her Age

HERE LYETH
Y⁰ BODY OF W . . .
REVE WHO D . . .
IN THE 49 YEA .
OF HIS AGE DYED
APRIL Y⁰ 29 1697

IN MEMORY of Mʳ
SAMUEL REEVE
who departed
this Life April the
15ᵗʰ A.D. 1768 Aged
63 Years 3 M⁰ and
22 Days

In Memory of
Mʳ SAMUEL TERRY
who departed this
life Augˢᵗ y⁰ 13 1762
Aged 69 Years
5 Months & 6 days

In Memory of Benjamin yᵉ Son of Jofhua & Mary Reve he died Octʳ 23ᵈ 1772 Aged 2 Years & 3 Mᵒ.

In Memory of Abigail the Daughter of Jofhua & Mary Reve died Octobʳ 7ᵗʰ 1772 Aged 9 Years. But Jefus called them unto him.

In Memory of Mary Daughter of Jofhua & Mary Reve died Octobʳ 8ᵗʰ 1772 in the 7ᵗʰ Year of her Age.

In Memory of Ketury Daughter of Jofhua & Mary Reve died Octobʳ 3ᵈ 1772 aged 4 Years & 4 Mᵒ.

In Memory of Mary Daughter of Jofhua & Mary Reve died April 1ˢᵗ 1764 aged 3 Years.

HERE LYES THE
BODY OF
Mʳ JOSEPH REEVE
AGED 80 YEARS
DECᴰ APRIL Yᵉ 22ᴰ
1 7 3 6

Here lyes yᵉ Body of
Mʳˢ Elizabeth Reve
Wife to Mʳ William
Reve Who Died
Janʳʸ yᵉ 13ᵗʰ 1738–9 in yᵉ
40 Year of her Age

In Memory of
Mary yᵉ Wife of Mʳ
John Youngs
who died Octobʳ
17ᵗʰ A.D. 1764
Aged 66 Years

In Memory of
Mr. John Overton
who died
July 20ᵗʰ AD 1794
in the 59ᵗʰ year
of his age
My flefh fhall flumber in
the ground
Till the laft trumpet's joyful
found
Then burft the chains with
fweet furprife
And in my Saviour's image
rife

Here lyes yᵉ Body of
Mary Reeve Daugᵗʳ
of Mʳ Benjamin &
Mʳˢ Deliverance
Reeve Who Died
Novʳ 7ᵗʰ 1740 Aged
15 Years 3 Monˢ & 14 Dˢ

In Memory of
Mʳ William Booth
Son of Lieuᵗ Conftant
& Mʳˢ Mary Booth
Who died March 12ᵗʰ
A.D. 1760 in yᵉ 33ᵈ
year of his Age
May Angels guard thy Duft
Untill the Meeting of yᵉ Juft

In
Memory of
Mrs. ANNE WELLS,
Wife of
Deac. Fregift Wells,
who died
June 15, 1793,
in the 73 year
of her age.

HERE LIES BURIED
THE BODY OF
Lʏᴅɪᴀ Gᴏʟᴅsᴍɪᴛʜ
ᴅᴀᴜ ᴏꜰ Lɪᴇᴜⁿᵗ
Jᴏʜɴ Gᴏʟᴅsᴍɪᴛʜ
& Mʳˢ Bᴇᴛʜɪᴀʜ ʜɪs ᴡɪꜰᴇ
AGED 20 YEARS
2 Mᵒ & 11 Dˢ DIED
DECᴿ 27ᵗʰ 1753

In Memory of
Mrs. Bethiah
Goldfmith Wife
of Lieuᵗ John
Goldfmith
who died
June 21ˢᵗ 1755
in the 48ᵗʰ year
of her age

Here lyes ye Body
of Benjamin Reeve
Son of Mr Benjamin
& Mrs Deliverance
Reeve Who Died Nov^{br}
ye 17 1740 Aged 21
Years 7 Mont^s & 25 D^s

In Memory of Enfign
BENJAMIN REEVS
Who Died May ye 18th
Old Stile 1752 in y^e
66th Year of His Age

ABIGAL HUBBARD DAU
TO CAP^T JSAAC &
Mrs BETHIAH HUBBARD
AGED 7 WEEKS & 1 DAY
DEC^D FEB Y^e 19th
1 7 3 2–3

In Memory of Jeremiah
Goldfmith Son of Lieu^t
John & Mrs Bethiah
Goldfmith Died Octo^r
21st 1753 Aged 5
Years 6 Mon^s 24 D^s.

HERE LYES THE
BODY OF Mr JOHN
GOOLDSMITH AGED
44 YEARS DEC^D
MARCH THE 1st
1 7 2 4

In Memory of
Lieu^t John
Goldfmith
who died
Septr 18th 1779
in the 75th year
of his age

Here lyes Buried
ye Body of M^{rs}
BETHIAH STEER
Widdow, Who Died
Octo^{br} 11th *Anno Domⁱ*
1739 in ye 67th Year
of Her Age

HERE LYES Y^e BODY
OF BETHIAH REEUE
WIFE OF THOMAS
REEUE AGED 26
YEARS AND 5
MONTHS DIED FEB^{ry}
Y^e 3 1713–4

Here lies
Interr'd the Body
of Mr Amafa Pike
he Departed this
life Auguft ye 24th
1756 in ye 28th year
of his Age

Here lieth Interr'd
the Body of Major
John Salmon who
was Born Novem^r y^e
19th 1698 & Departed
this Life July ye 28th
1762 in the 64th
Year of his Age

Here lies Interr'd
the Body of M^r
William Salmon
Who Departed
this Life May
the 10th A.D. 1759
in the 75 year
of his Age

In Memory of Mrs. Lydia Salmon, the *Virtuous* Wife of Maj^r John Salmon, who following the Example of her Hufband, gave her eftate to the fupport of the Gofpel in this Parifh. She departed this Life April 4th 1776, Aged 78 Years.

Here lyes ye Body
of Mrs HANNAH
SALMON, Wife to M^r
WILLIAM SALMON
Who Died Feb^{ry} 2^d
1750–1 Aged 67 Years
5 Months & 5 Days

Here lyes Buried y^e
Body of ye Widdow
SARAH SALMON Who
Departed this life
Nov^{br} 3rd 1758 in y^e
83rd Year of her Age.

In Memory of Jofeph Halliock, Son of Mr Jofeph & Mrs Abigail Halliock who departed this Life May 30th A.D. 1779, Aged 15 years, 2 months & 15 days.

In Memory of Jofhua Halliock, Son of Mr Jofeph & Mrs Abigail Halliock, who departed this Life Jan^ry 16th A.D. 1787, Aged 16 years, 10 months & 3 days.

In Memory of Mrs Bethiah Halliock, Wife of Mr Benjamin Halliock who departed this Life April 9th A.D. 1780, Aged 24 years, 5 months & 15 days.

ZACCHEUS
GOLDSMITH
AGED 21 YEARS
& 2 M^o & 9 DAYS
DIED JAN^ry Y^e 22^D
1706-7.

In
Memory of
Deacon
FREEGIFT WELLS
who died Nov^br 26th
1785 in the 72^d Year
of his Age
& 15th of his office.
True peace with God & me he ere purfued
He fought the Church's weal his neighbor's good,
The loving parent & to Chrift a Friend,
Serene in Life & peaceful was his End

Here
lies the
Body of M^rs
Keturah the wife of
Mr Thomas wells
fhe died March ye 9th
1764 in the 20th year
of her Age.

Mary the
Daughter of M^r
Fregift and M^rs
Anna Wells died
July ye 8th 1753
Aged 1 year & 5 M^t.

In Memory of
Mary ann Daugh^r
of Jonathan &
Alethea Tuthill
who died
Auguft 24th 1794
aged 8 years
& 14 days.

In Memory of
Jonathan H. Son
of Jonathan &
Anne Tuthill
who died
Decr 19th 1785
aged 6 years, 1
month & 1 day.

In Memory of Henry, Son of Jonathan & Alethea Tuthill, who died Auguft 16th, 1785, aged 1 year & 5 months.

In Memory of
JOSHUA WELLS
who died February
6th 1787 in the
44 Year of his
Age.

Near Here Lyes The Body of
MR William Wells The Oldest
Son of William Wells, Esqr
Who Departed This Life In
October 1696 Aged About
37 Years.

In Memory of
David Son of
Doc^t David &
Mrs Lydia Conkling who died
Jany 20th 1779 in
the 2^d Year of
his Age.

HERE LIES THE BODY
OF Mrs MARY WIGGINS
THE WIFE OF M^r
JOHN WIGGINS JUN^r
WHO DEPARTED THIS
LIFE JULY Y^e 3^D
1749
AGED 21 YEARS & 7 M^o.

WELLS OF SOVTH HOLD GEN^T JVSTICE OF Y^e PEACE & FIRSt

HERE LIES Y^e BODY OF WILLIAM

SHERIFFE OF NEW YORKE SHIRE

Yea here hee lies who speaketh yet though dead

on wings of Faith his soule to Heauen is fled

His pious Deedes And charity was svch

That of his praise no pen can write too much

As was his Life so was his bleft Deceafe

Hee Liud in Loue And sweetly dyd in peace

VPON LONG ISLAND WHO DEPARTED THIS LIFE NOVE 18th 1671 AGED 63

Here lyes ye Body of
Mr SAMUEL WINDES
Who died Nov^{br} 25th
1739 Aged 56 Years
6 Months & 20 Day^s.

HERE LYES BURIED
THE BODY OF
Mr ISAAC OVERTON
AGED 28 YEARS
DEC^D MARCH Y^e
1 7 4 0

In Memory of
Mrs Alethea y^e
wife of Mr Nath^{ll}
Overton who
died Dec^ember
ye 24th 1753 in
ye 44th year
of her Age

In Memory of
Decⁿ James Cor^win
who died
June 24th 1796
aged 55 years

In Memory of M^r
Lazrus Horton
who died Sep^t
9th 1764
in the 40th year
of his Age

In Memory of MEHETABLE
SAWYER Confort of MOSES
SAWYER & Daug^{tr} of Mr JONATHAN
& Mrs MARY HORTON Who
Died April ye 21st 1751 Aged
19 Years 1 Month & 25 Days
Behold all you who do pafs by
As you are now fo once was I
As I am now fo you muft be
Prepare for death and follow me

BODY OF CAPTAIN JOHN CONKELYNE BORNE

HERE LYETH THE   LIFE THE SIXT   DAY OF APRILL   ATT SOVTH HOLD   ON LONG ILAND IN   THE SIXTY FOVRTH   YEAR OF HIS   AGE ANNO DOM   1694   IN NOTTINGHAM

SHIP IN ENGLAND WHO DEPARTED THIS

In Memory of
David Son
of Jofeph &
Deliverance
Horton he
died Sep^tr
7th 1772 in
the 9th Year
of his Age

In Memory of
Mr Daniel Tuthill
who died Novr 18th
1768 in the 57th
year or his Age
Children and friends
Come view my Grave
receive God's Chrift
& heaven have.

Mehetabel
Daughter of
Lazarus &
Anna Horton
died July 9th 1773
in her 16th Year.

DANIEL TUTTLE
or &c. Aged 13 Years
Lacking 3 Months &
2 Days as it is faid
Died Septr 8th 1752.

LYDIA TUTHILL DAU^r
TO Mr DANIEL & M^rs
MEHETABLE TUTHILL
DIED NOV^R 5th
1738 AGED 8
WEEKS & 5 D^s.

In Memory of M
Mehetable Tuthill
Wife of Mr Daniel
Tuthill who died
Novr 27th 1788
Aged 73 Years
Our age to Seventy
Years is fet
How fhort the term
how frail the state

In Memory of M^rs
Mehetabel Horton
the Virtuous
Wife of Capt
Benjamin Horton
who departed this
Life Octr 16th
AD 1787 Aged
25 years 1 month
& 14 days

In Memory of Capt
Barnabas Horton
who departed this
Life April 17th
AD. 1787
Aged 61 years
& 6 months

In
Memory of
Anna, daugh^r of
Capt. Barnabas &
Susanna Horton
who died
April 1781
aged 22 years

In Memory of Rhoda, Daughter of Jonathan & Alethea Tuthill, who died Decr 4th 1790, aged 9 years, 9 months & 3 days.

HERE LYES Y^e BODY OF BETHIA HORTON DAU^r TO JAMES & ANNA HORTON AGED 8 M^o & 26 DAYES DEC^d MARCH Y^e 27th 1722. Here lyes her body in the duft to be raifd at ye Resurection of ye Juft.

HERE LIES THE BODY OF ANNA HAUGHTON DAU^r OF Mr JAMES & Mrs ANNA HAUGHTON DIED DEC^R 3^D 1753 AGED 13 YEARS 1 M^o & 10 D^s.

IN MEMORY of
Deacon James Horton
who died May ye 16th
A.D. 1762 in the
68th Year of his Age.

Intomb'd beneath this ponderous heavy Load
Lies the Man who lov'd & fear'd the Lord
A Hufband dear, a Father ever kind;
To Minifters a clofe and conftant Friend.
Sober, Blamelefs to Charity inclin'd
Meriting well of All he left behind

HERE LYES BURIED
Y^e BODY OF
CALEB HORTON
AGED 30 YEARS
1 M^o & 14 D^s
DIED DECR Y^e 25th
1 7 0 6

In Memory of
Mrs Anna Horton
W^{do} of Deacⁿ
James Horton
who departed this
Life March 8th
AD. 1783 Aged
82 years 2 months
& 6 days

IN MEMORY of
MEHETABEL ye Wife
of WILLIAM HORTON
She died March y^e
21st 1772 in the
62nd Year of her Age
She was kind to all a
Friend to all & belov'd
of all

In Memory of
Dea^c
William Horton
who died Sep^t 26
1788 in the 80th
Year of his
Age

In Memory of
Mrs Patience
Horton Wife of M^r
William Horton
who died June 27th
1786 in the 47th
Year of her age

In Memory of
Mr.
Sylvester
L'Hommedieu
who departed this
Life March 9, 1788
in the 86th Year
of his Age

In Memory of
M^{RS} SUSANNA
L'HOMMEDIEU
who died Feb^y
10th 1774 in
the 26 Year of
her Age

10

HERE LYETH BURIED THE BODY OF

(left margin, vertical): SOUTH-HOLD THE 13 DAY OF JULY 1680 AGED 80 YEARS

(right margin, vertical): MR BARNABAS HORTON BORN AT MOUSLLY IN LESTERSHIRE IN

HERE SLEPES MY BODY TOMBED IN ITS DUST
TILL CHRIST SHALL COME & RAISE IT WITH THE JUST
MY SOUL'S ASSENDED TO THE THRONE OF GOD
WHERE WITH SWEET JESUS NOW I MAKE ABOAD
THEN HASTEN AFTER ME MY DEAREST WIFE
TO BE PERTAKER OF THIS BLESSED LIFE
AND YOU DEAR CHILDREN ALL FOLLOW THE LORD
HEAR & OBEY HIS PUBLICK SACRED WORD
AND IN YOUR HOUSES CALL UPON HIS NAME
FOR OFT I HAUE ADVIS'D YOU TO THE SAME
THEN GOD WILL BLESS YOU WITH YOUR CHILDREN ALL
AND TO THIS BLESSED PLACE HE WILL YOU CALL
HEBREWS H & Y^e 4
HE BEING DEAD YET SPEAKETH

Alfo at his feet lie the remains of his youngest

son

Jonathan Horton

the first Captain of Cavalry

in the County of Suffolk

He died Feb. 23 AD. 1707. Æ. 60.

(bottom margin, inverted): OLD ENGLAND & DYED AT

HERE LYES Y^e BODY
OF HENRY CASE
DIED APRIL Y^e
16th 1 7 2 0
IN Y^e 36th YEAR
OF HIS AGE.

HERE LIES Y^e BODY OF JAMES CASE DIED SEP^t Y^e 12th 1753 AGED 11 YEARS & 1 M^o. ALSO AZUBAH CASE DIED NOV^R Y^e 12th 1753 AGED 6 YEARS & 8 M^o. SON & DAU^R OF MR WILLIAM & Mrs ANNA CASE

In Memory of *Francis*, son of *Matthias & Julia* Case; who died Nov. 18, 1799 Æ 2 years & 4 days

IN MEMORY OF LUTHER CASE SON OF M^R. MOSES & M^rs. MARY CASE DIED JAN^ry. 29th 1755 AGED 4 YEARS 11 MONTHS & 22 D^s.

11

Mary the Daughter of Mofes & Mary Cafe died May 7th 1764 Aged 9 Years 5 M° & 27 Days

Martha the Daughter of Mofes and Mary Cafe died May 17th 1764 Aged 2 Years 8 M° & 25 Days

In Memory of Mrs Mary Cafe Wife of Lt Mofes Case who died Jan^{ry} 21st AD. 1783 in the 56th year of her Age

In Memory of M^{rs}
BETHIAH VAIL Wife to
MR JEREMIAH VAIL
Who Died July ye 26th
1753   Aged 22 Years
7 Months & 22 Days

[On three sides of a modern white marble monument.]

IN MEMORY OF PHILEMON DICKERSON, OR DICKINSON, WHO WITH HIS BROTHERS NATHANIEL AND JOHN DICKINSON, EMIGRATED FROM ENGLAND AND LANDED IN MASSACHUSETTS IN 1638. HE WAS ADMITTED A FREEMAN OF THE TOWN OF SALEM IN 1641, AND REMOVED TO SOUTHHOLD L.I. IN 1646, WHERE HE DIED IN 1672 AGED ABOUT 74 YEARS, LEAVING TWO SONS, THOMAS AND PETER.

IN MEMORY OF PETER DICKERSON WHO WAS BORN IN 1648 & DIED IN 1721 AGED ABOUT 73 YEARS, LEAVING TWO SONS JOHN AND THOMAS.

IN MEMORY OF THOMAS DICKERSON WHO DIED IN THE YEAR 1724 AGED ABOUT 53 YEARS LEAVING FOUR SONS, THOMAS, JOSHUA, DANIEL & PETER, ALL OF WHOM REMOVED TO MORRIS COUNTY, STATE OF NEW JERSEY ABOUT THE YEAR 1745.

Here lyes ye Body
of Abigail Windes
Dau^{tr} of Mr Samu^{el}
Windes Who Died
Nov^{br} 21st 1739 Aged
13 Years & 28 Days

Here lyes ye Body
of Abner Windes
Son of Mr Samuel
Windes Who Died
Nov^{br} 20th 1739 Aged
19 Years 10 M° & 7 D^s.

HERE LIES Y^e BODY OF
PARNAL VAILL
DAU^R OF M^r
PETER & M^{rs}
BETHIAH VAILL
DIED JULY 25th 1753
AGED 8 MONTHS
WANTING 5 DAYS

IN MEMORY OF
Mr JOSHUA DRAKE
SON OF M^r
FRANCIS & M^{rs}
PHEBE DRAKE
AGED 34 YEARS
2 M° & 19 D^s DIED
AUG^t 8th 1755

HERE LYETH BURIE^D
Y^e BODY OF MARY
VAILE AGED 39
YEARS DEPARTED
THIS LIFE Y^e 22
OF SEPTEMBER
1 6 8 9

HERE LYES Y^e BODY
OF ENSIGN RICHARD
TERRY DEC^d FEB^{ry}
Y^e 2^D 1 7 2 3
IN Y^e 64th YEAR
OF HIS AGE

HERE LYES Y^e BODY
OF Mr JEREMIAH
VAIL AGED 77
YEARS DEC^D NOV^R
Y^e 28th 1 7 2 6

HERE LYES BURIED
THE BODY OF
Mrs BETHIAH HORTON WIFE TO
CAP^t JONATHAN HORTON
DEC^D APRIL Y^e 14th 1733
IN Y^e 80th YEAR
OF HER AGE

This monument is erected
to the Memory *of*
TIMOTHY H. BIGELOW
of Middleton in Connecticut
who died at this place
Auguft 7th 1791 in the
29th year of his Age

In Memory of M^r
Jonathan Horton
who died April 3^d
1 7 6 8
in the 85th year
of his Age

HERE LYES BURIED
THE BODY OF
Mr THOMAS REEVE
AGED 59 YEARS
DIED NOV^r Y^e 9th
1 7 3 8

HERE LYES Y^e BODY
OF BETHIAH REEVE
AGED 15 YEARS
& 7 DAYS DIED
MARCH 1st 1739

Sacred
to the Memory of
Mrs CHARITY L'HOMMEDIEU
the amiable & pious wife of the
Honble EZRA L'HOMMEDIEU, Efquire,
who departed this Life July 31, 1785,
in the 46 Year of her Age,
This monument is erected.
The House appointed for all living
when the dread Trumpet sounds the slumbering Duft but
not inattentive to the call shall wake
nor shall the conscious soul amidft the Crowd
mistake its Partner — Thricè happy meeting,
nor Time nor Death shall ever part them more.

In Memory of
the Honorable
EZRA L'HOMMEDIEU Esq.
who
having through a long life
faithfully served in the
councils of his country
during
the arduous struggle
of the revolution
and the calm of
Independence
died Sept. 27, 1811
Æ. 77.

Here
lies the
Body of M^r
Nathan Halluck he
died Decr 2nd 1756 in the
28 year of his age
truft not to flattering
prospects, O be wife;
nor hope for happinefs
below the fkise

In Memory of M^{rs}
Deborah Landon
wife of Jared
Landon Efq^r
who died July 9th
AD. 1779
Aged 35 years

In Memory of
Samuel Landon, Efq^r
who died Jan^{ry} 21st
1 7 8 2
Aged 82 years
& 8 months

HERE LYES Y^e BODY
OF NATHAN LANDON
AGED 54 YEARS
DIED MARCH Y^e 9th
1 7 1 8

IN MEMORY
of Bethiah the
Virtuous Wife of
Samuel Landon Efq^r
who died Auguft 30th
A.D. 1761 in the
58th Year of her Age

HERE LIES THE
BODY OF M^{rs}
PARNAL LANDON
WHO DEPARTED
THIS LIFE JAN^{RY} Y^e
16th 1750 ⁄ 51
AGED 49 YEARS

HERE LYETH Y^e
BODY OF
HANNAH LANDON
WIFE TO NATHAN
LANDON AGED
30 YEARS DEC^D
FABUARY Y^e 26
1 7 0 1

In Memory of
Mrs.
MARTHA LANDON
Late Confort of
JARED LANDON *Efq^r*
who departed this
Life 26 of April AD.
1775 aged 34 Years
& ten Months.

HERE
LIETH THE BODY
OF HANNAH GRIFFING
WIFE OF JASPER
GRIFFING BORN AT
MANCHESTER IN NEW
ENGLAND AGED 46 YEARES
AND 8 DAYES AND WAS
MOTHER OF 14 CHILDREN
AND DEPARTED THIS LIFE
IN SOVTHOLD THE 20
DAY OF APRIL 1699

Here lies
Interr'd the Body
of Mrs Elifebeth
Griffing the wife
of Mr Sam^{ll} Griffing
who died Auguft
9th 1755 . . [broken] . .
year of her Age

Aaron
the fon of M^r
Samuel and M^{rs}
Elifebeth Griffing
died October y^e
21st 1754 in y^e [illeg.]rd
year of his Age

Parnal
daughter of M^r
Samuel and M^{rs}
Martha Griffing
fhe died July
29 1764 in her
5th year

In Memory
of Lydia Daughter
of Mr Samuel and
Mrs Elifebeth
Griffing fhe died
October ye 12th 1754
in ye 17th year of
her Age

Here Lyes Buried
ye Body of Mr
ROBERT GRIFFIN
Who Decd March
ye 27th 1729 Aged
43 Years

Here lyes ye Body of
Mrs LYDIA CONKLING
Wife to Lieut JOSEPH
CONKLING Who Died
Janry 27th *Anno Domi*
1742 ∕ 3 Aged 57 Years

HERE LYES BURIED Ye
BODY OF MR RICHARD
STEER CITIZEN OF LONDON
WHO DEPARTED THIS
LIFE JUNE Ye 20th 1721 IN
Ye 78 YEAR OF HIS AGE

IN MEMORY
of Elizabeth the Wife
of Doctr Samuel Gelfton
who died July ye 10th A.D.
1760 Aged 35 Years &
4 Months

In Memory of
JAMES the Son
of Mr JOSEPH and
Mrs MARGRET LANDON
who died AUGst 26th 1756
in 13th Year of his Age

In Memory of
JOSEPH the Son
of Mr JOSEPH and
Mrs MARGRET LANDON
Died AUGst 16th 1756
in the 13th Year of his Age

HERE LIES Ye BODY OF NATHAN LANDON SON OF Mr JOSEPH &
Mrs MARGRETT LANDON AGED 2 YEARS & 18 Ds DIED SEPt 14th 1754

HERE LIES Ye BODY OF GLORIANNAR LANDON DAUr OF Mr JOSEPH
& Mrs MARGRETT LANDON AGED 6 YEARS & 2 Mo DIED SEPt 7th 1754.

Anna ye Daught'r of Joseph & Margaret Landon died Augt 16, 1747 aged 1
Year 5 Mo & 20 Days.

HERE LYES Ye
BODY OF Mrs
MARY LANDON
WIFE TO IAMES LANDON
DECD AUGUST
Ye 28 1 7 2 2
IN Ye [blank]
YEAR OF HER AGE

In Memory of
Efther Daughter
of Hazard L. &
Efther Moore
who died
Novr 16th 1794
aged 21 days

HERE LYES Ye
BODY OF Mr
THOMAS MOORE
WHO DYED DECr
Ye 30th 1738
IN Ye 76 YEAR
OF HIS AGE

HERE LYES Ye BODY OF
Mrs JANE MOORE
WIFE OF Mr THOMAS
MOORE WHO DYED
NOVr Ye 28 1756
IN Ye 60 YEAR
OF HER AGE

HERE LYES THE BODY
OF DEBORAH MOORE
DAUr TO Mr THOMAS & Mrs
JANE MOORE DECD SEPr
Ye 7th 1736 IN THE
34 YEAR OF HER AGE

MARY PAIN THE
WIF OF IOHN PAIN
WAS BORN 26 OF
MAY 1661 DEYED
SEPTEMBR 25
1690

IOHN ALLSVP
BORN JANʳʸ Yᵉ 3ᵈ 61
DECEASED JVNE 4ᵗʰ
1 6 9 4

Mʳ
DANIEL ALLSVP
BORN AVGˢᵗ Yᵉ 13ᵗʰ
67 DECEASED
11 of JANVARY
1 6 9 8

Interred is the Remains of JOHN GELSTON SON of DOCᵗʳ SAM. GELS-
TON & ELIZABETH HIS WIFE who departed this Life Augᵗ 25ᵗʰ 1756 Æ 1
Year & 10 Dˢ

Elizabeth yᵉ Daughter of Samuel & Elizabeth Gelfton died May 17ᵗʰ 1760 Aged
2 Years & 3 Months.

HER : LYETH : THE : BO=
DY : OF : LIDIA GRIFF=
ING : WHO : DESESED
APRIL : THE : 2=1718=IN
THE : 9 : Yʳ : OF : HER : AGE

HERE LYES Yᵉ BODY
OF JASPER GRIFFING
DIED APRIL Yᵉ 17ᵗʰ
1718 IN Yᵉ 70 YEAR
OF HIS AGE

The Remains of Mʳˢ
Eunic Storrs Daughtʳ
of yᵉ Honorabˡᵉ Shubˡ
Conant Efqʳ of Manf
field & Wife to yᵉ Revᵈ
John Storrs, Paftor of
yᵉ firft Church of
CHRIST in Southold
Who died March 27
A.D. 1767 Aged 31 year

In Memory of
Capᵗ John Prince
who Departed
this Life Janrʸ
24ᵗʰ 1765 Aged
77 Years 2 Mᵒ
and 3 Days

In Memory of
Relyanc yᵉ Wife
of Capᵗ John
Prince who died
June 5ᵗʰ 1761
in the 30ᵗʰ Year
of her Age

Sacred to the *Memory*
of Mrs. Martha Horton
the *amiable & pious*
Wife of Lieuᵗ William
Horton who departed
Nov. 10th 1793
this life in the 34th
year of her age

In Memory of
Daniel Son of
Mr. Jofiah &
Mrs. Elizabeth
Woodhull
who died
July 2ᵈ 1793
aged 5 years
& 5 days

In Memory of Mʳˢ
ELIZABETH BUDD Wife to
Mʳ JOHN BUDD formerly
Wife to yᵉ Honbˡᵉ SAMUEL
HUTCHINSON Efqʳ Who
Died April yᵉ 11ᵗʰ 1751 in
yᵉ 71 Year of Her Age

HERE LYES Yᵉ BODY OF
MARY HUCHINSON
WIFE TO MATHIAS
HUCHINSON AGED 47
YEARS 2 Mᵒ & 9 Dˢ
DECᴰ FEBʳʸ Yᵉ 22ᴰ
1721–22

16

HERE LYES
Yᵉ BODY OF
ELISHA MAROW
WHO DIED IVLY
4 1724 IN THE 23
YEAR OF HIS AGE

TO THE BLESSED MEMORY
OF Mᴿˢ MARY HOBART
BORN AT BOSTON
WHO AFTER SHE HAD
SERVED IN HER OWNE
AGE BY THE WILL OF
GOD FELL ON SLEEP
IN THIS PLACE THE
19 OF APRIL
1 6 9 8
AGED 56 YEARS 1 MONTH
AND 7 DAYS
DESIRD SHE LIVD
LAMENTED SHE DID
DYE YET STILL SHE
LIVES IN PRECIOVS
MEMORY
MY SOVLE ASCENDS
ABOVE THE STARS

In Memory of
The Revᵈ Mʳ WILLIAM
THROOP who departed this
Life Septʳ 29 A.D. 1756
Aged 36 Years & 3 Months

IN MEMORY OF DANIEL RUTHERFORD SON OF THE REVᴰ Mᴿ
WILLᴹ & Mᴿˢ MERCY THROOP WHO DEPARTED THIS LIFE JUNᴱ
Yᴱ 17ᵗʰ 1754 AGED 5 MONTHS & 17 DAYS. Here Death proclaims how
Infants fell when Man became an Heir of Hell.

HERE LYES Yᵉ BODY
OF MARTHA HUCHINSᴼᴺ
AGED 9 YEARS 8 Mᴼ
& 18 DAYES DIED
SEPTᴿ Yᵉ 18 DAY 1717

HERE LYES Yᵉ BODY
OF Mʳ MATTHIAS
HUTCHINSON DECᴰ
JANʳʸ Yᵉ 16ᵗʰ 1723–4
IN Yᵉ 36ᵗʰ YEAR
OF HIS AGE

HERE LYES BURIED
Yᵉ BODY OF SAMUEL
HUTCHINSON AGED
16 YEARS AND
2 MONTHS
DYED MAY Yᵉ
24 1 7 1 7

Here lyes yᵉ Body
of Mʳ THOMAS
HUTCHINSON Who
Died Janʳʸ 8ᵗʰ 1748/9 in
yᵉ 83ᵈ Year of his Age

Here lyes Interred yᵉ
Body of yᵉ Honᵇˡ Coˡˡ
SAMUEL HUTCHINSON
Efqʳ Who Departed this
life Janʳʸ 9ᵗʰ 1737 in yᵉ
65ᵗʰ Year of His Age

In Memory of
Mr MATTHIAS HUTCHINSON
who departed this Life on
the 17th day of JANUARY A.D.
1759 Aged 23 Years & 29 Days
He with his Anceftors had Virtue all
But he alone in prime of Life muft fall
By Death to end the Illuftrious Line
It muft be so & we to Heaven refign

In Memory of Collo
ELIJAH HUTCHINSON Efqr
Who Departed this Life
Octor ye 15th 1754 Aged 55
Years 11 Months & 25 Ds
Peace was the lovely object he perfu'd
He fought ye Churches Weal his Neigh-
bors good
And now at Large we trust he shares
above
Unfullied Peace & Everlafting love
Math. v. 9. Blefsed are ye Peace makers

In Memory of
Mrs. MARY, Relict of
Col. Elijah Hutchinson
who died
April 9th, 1783,
in the 70th year
of her age

In Memory of
Lydia Paine Daur
of Mr Allfup & Mrs
Phebe Paine, Who
Died Novbr 2nd 1750
Aged 15 Years 1
Month & 20 Days

IN MEMORY of
Hannah Wife of Docr
Samuel Hutchinfon
who died Feby 6th 1760
in ye 24th Year of Her Age
Nor Virtue, Youth or
Godlinefs could Save
The Loving Wife and Parent
from the Grave;
Cropp'd like a Rose before 'tis
fully blown,
She ended Life, nor half Her
Worth was known.

HERE LYES Ye BODY OF
MARTHA Ye WIFE OF
IOHN PECK WHO
DYED MAY Ye 29
1725 AGED 55 Y

Here lieth ye Body
of Frances ye
Daughter of John
& Efther Peck
died May ye 16
1738 In ye 5th
year of her age

IÕ P
1712

Io P
1715
ye 6

[The above are two stones, probably, of Pecks. They are of brown stone, very rudely cut and badly weathered. The dates uncertain, may be 1772 and 1775. Remaining portions of original inscriptions, if any, are now obliterated.]

In Memory of
Mr Jofeph Peck
who died June
28th 1789 in the
51ft Year
of her Age

In Memory of
Mrs Lucretia Peck
Wife of Mr
Jofeph Peck
who died Sepr 4th
1773 in the 33d
Year of her age

In
Memory of
SYLVANUS DAVIS
who died May 13th
1781, aged 83
years.

IN MEMORY OF
Mrs MARY DAVIS
WIFE OF M^r
SYLVANUS DAVIS
WHO DEPARTED THIS
LIFE SEP^t THE 26th
1 7 5 4
AGED 58 YEARS
7 MONTHS & 9 D^s

In Memory of
Mrs MARY DAVIS
Dau^r of Mr SYLVANUS
& Mrs MARY DAVIS
who died Septr the
26th 1 7 6 3
Aged 32 Years
7 Months & 28 days

In Memory of
Mary the Wife of
Mr Silvanus Davis
& Daughter of M^r
Cartrett & Mrs Mary
Gilliam who died
July the 28th 1771
In the 71th Year
of her Age

Here lies Interr'd
the Body of
David Corey Efq^r
who Departed
this life Octob^r
ye 30th A.D. 1758
Aged 68 years
6 months and
14 Days

HERE LYETH
THE BODY OF
MARY CORY
WHO DIED DE
CEMBER 24th
1721 IN THE
30th YEAR OF
HER AGE

JAMES PERAZIM GILBOA MOORE, son to Mr MICAH and Mrs JERUSHA MOORE, who died AUG^t 29, 1756 Aged 1 Year 3 M^o & 6 D^s.

IN MEMORY of JULIANA MARGARITA MOORE, DAU^R of Mr MICAH & Mrs JERUSHA MOORE DIED SEP^t 18th 1754 AGED 8 YEARS 5 MONTHS & 5 DAYS.

IN MEMORY of JAMES MOORE SON OF Mr MICAH & Mrs JERUSHA MOORE DIED AUG^t 2^D 1754 AGED 4 YEARS 8 MONTHS & 10 D^s.

IN MEMORY OF BENJAMIN MOORE SON OF Mr MICAH & Mrs JERUSHA MOORE DIED AUG^t 2^D 1754 AGED 2 YEARS 4 MONTHS & 22 D^s.

IN MEMORY OF JOSHUA MOORE SON OF Mr MICAH & Mrs JERUSHA MOORE DIED JULY 30th 1754 AGED 6 MONTHS & 20 D^s.

IN MEMORY OF PERAZIM GILBOA MOORE SON OF Mr MICAH & M^r. JERUSHA MOORE DIED JULY 26th 1754 AGED 6 YEARS 5 MONTHS & 10 D^s.

Jerufha, Daughter of Micah & Jerufha Moore, died Novem^r 6th 1747 aged 6 Years 2 M^o & 9 Days.

Frances, Daught'r of Micah & Jerufha Moore, died Octob^r 8th 1747 aged 4 Years & 7 M^o & 29 Days.

Eunice, Daught'r of Micah & Jerufh Moore, died Novem 19 1747 aged 3 Years 1 M° & 11 Days.

MARTHA, Daughter of Simon & Abigail More died Sept' 21, 1758 Aged 13 years 5 mo.

ABIGAIL, Daughter of Simon & Abigail More died Sept' 10 1758 Aged 1? years 8 mo^{ts}.

ABIGAIL
Wife of Simon
MORE Died July
21ᶠᵗ 1758 Aged
45 Years &
11 Months

MARY
Wife of Stephen
Halfey Died Augst
15 1758 Aged
20 Years

In Memory of
Mrs Ann Moore
Wife of M^r
Simon Moore
who died Sep^t 28th
AD. 1778
in the 56th year
of her Age

In
Memory of
HANNAH, Wife of
SIMON MOORE
who died
Octr 13th 1796,
aged 66 years

In
Memory of
SIMON MOORE
who died March 12th
1802 aged 84 years

In Memory of
Elizabeth Drummy Howard
Daughter of Revd Jofeph
& Mrs Jane Hazard
who died
June 1st 1800!
aged 16 days

IN MEMORY of
Mr Smith Stratton
M.A. who departed
this life March 10th
A.D. 1758 in y^e
31ᶠᵗ Year of his Age

Beneath this duft lie the remains of
the Rev. ELAM POTTER
a faithful good minifter of Jefus Chrift
He died Jan^r 5th Aged 52
in the year 1794
Forbear to weep my loving friends
Death is the voice Jehovah sends
To call us to our home;
Through thefe dark fhades from pains redreft
Is the right path to endlefs reft
Where joys immortal bloom.

In Memory of
WILLIAM BAKER
son of Mr BEZA & M^{rs}
MARY BAKER who was
born July ye 4th 1755
& died Octr ye 15, 1756.

Here lies
the Body of
Baze Baker he
died Feby the 26
1756 in the 32nd
year of his Age

HERE LYES BURIED
THE BODY OF M^{rs}
ELIZABETH YOUNGS WIFE
TO BENJAMIN YOUNGS ESQ^r
DEC^D JUNE Y^e 15 1735
IN Y^e 71st YEAR
OF HER AGE

In
Memory of
THOMAS CONKLIN
who died
March 4, 1782
aged 87 years

IN MEMORY
of Rachel ye Wife of
Mr Thomas Conklin
died May ye 10th 1750
in ye 46 year
of his Age

In
Memory of
JERUSHA Daughter
of Mr. Thomas & Mrs.
Eunice Hempfted
who died April 10th
1792 Aged 18 Years

In Memory of
Mrs KEZIA HEMPSTED Wife
of M^r. JOSHUA HEMPSTED
who departed this Life
OCT^r 3^d. A.D. 1756,
in the 27th Year of her Age.
"Behold the Bridegroom cometh."

D : H
1747

R : H
1746

[These are two stones, rough, and rudely lettered, probably of Hempsteads.]

In Memory of
MARY BAKER
Dau^r of Mr BEZA &
Mrs MARY BAKER who
was born Octr. ye 11, 1751
& died Octr. ye 18, 1756.

Here lies the Body
of Mr JOSEPH
BAKER Who Died
December ye 26th
A.D. 1761 In ye 74th
Year of His Age

Here lies the
Body of M^{rs} ANN
Wife of Mr Jofeph
Baker Who Died
January ye 8th
A D 1761 In the
66th Year of her
Age

In Memory of
REJOICE, *Daughter of*
Dr. John & M^{rs}. Abigail
Gardiner who died
Octr. 18th 1790,
Aged 7 Years, 3 months
and 2 days.*

In Memory of
Doct^r Micah Moore
who died Jan. 25th
1776 aged 62 Years
The graves of all
    the Saints he blest,
And soften'd every bed;
Where should the dieing
    members rest?
But with there living head.

* Near by are stones to the memory of Dr. John Gardiner, died Oct. 21, 1823, aged
71; of Abigail, his wife, died August 22, 1800, in her 36th year; of Margaret, his wife,
died Nov. 8, 1823, æ. 55.

ABIGAIL
MOORE AGED 10
YEARS DYED
Yᵉ 26 OF JUNE
1 6 8 2

ANAN MOORE
AGED 16 YEARS
DEPARTED THIS
LIFE AUGUST
Yᵉ 5 1 6 8 3

HERE LYES THE
BODY OF Mʳ
BENJAMIN MOORE
AGED 49 YEARS
AND 1 MONTH.
DYED JANUARY 27ᵗʰ
1 7 2 8

HERE LYES THE
BODY OF Mʳˢ
ABIGAIL MOORE
THE WIFE OF Mʳ.
BENJAMIN MOORE
AGED 70 YEARS &
4 Mᵒ DYED JUNE 20
1 7 4 6

In
Memory of
PHEBE, Wife of
ALLSUP PAINE
who died
Octʳ. 30, 1791,
aged 91 years.

ANNA
Daughter of
Mʀ *BENJAMIN*
AND
Mʀˢ *MARCY*
YOUNGS
died Janʳʸ 26ᵗʰ
174 [illeg.] Aged [illeg.] Years

BETHIAH yᵉ
WIFE OF THOMAS
GILBERT AGED 22 YĒRS
DECESED MAY 11ᵗʰ: 1684:
MOST PRESIOVS IN GODS SIGHᵗ
THE LORD DOTH AYE ESTEM
OF OVRS Yᵗ DYE IN CHRIST
WHAT EVER MEN DO DEMᵉ

HERE
LIETH THE
BODY OF DEBROAH
RAIYNER WHO
WAS BORN IN Yᵉ 28
OF APRIL 1690 WHO
DIED IVNE THE 27
1703 AGED 14
YEARS

HERE LYETH BURIEᴰ
Yᵉ BODY OF MARY
YOVNGS WIFE TO
THOMAS YOVNGS
AGED 19 YEARS &
MONTHES & 13
DAYES DIED Yᵉ 17
OF DECEMBER
1 6 8 7

HERE
LIETH IN
TERRED THE
BODY OF
COll THO
MAS YONGS
WHO DEPARTED
THIS LIFE JAN
UARY 27ᵗʰ 1714
IN THE 59
YEAR OF HIS
AGE

HERE LIETH INTERRED
THE BODY OF COLONELᴸ
IOHN YOVNGS ESQVIRE
LATE ONE OF HIS
MAIESTIES COVNCEL OF
THE PROVINCE OF
NEW YORK WHO
DEPARTED THIS LIFE
THE 12 DAY OF APRILL
ANNO DOMINI 1698
AGED 75 YEARS

HERE LYETH THE BODY
OF Mʀˢ MARY LYNDE
WIFE OF NATIHˡˡ LYNDE
ESQ^ʀ WHO WAS HER 3ᴰ
HVSBAND AND HER FIRST WAS
Mʀ PETER BRADLEY HER 2ᴰ
WAS Lᵀ COLL THOMAS
YOVNGS SHE DIED THE
4ᵗʰ OF IVLY 1724
AGED 67 YᵉARS

Here Lyes Buried
yᵉ Body of Mʳ.
Benjamin Youngs
Son of yᵉ Honourᵇˡᵉ
Benjamin Youngs
Esqʳ. & Mʳˢ. . . . . . His
Wife Who Died Sepᵗ
26ᵗʰ 1729 in yᵉ 27ᵗʰ
Year of His Age.

HERE LYES Yᵉ BODY
OF GROVER YOUNGS
SON OF BENJAMIN
YOUNGS ESQ^ᴿ & MARY
HIS WIFE WHO WAS
BORN IN SOUTHOLD
OCTᴿ Yᵉ 3ᴰ 1697
AND DIED JANʳʸ
Yᵉ 25ᵗʰ 1739/40.

Here lyes Interr'd yᵉ
Body of BENJAMIN
YOUNGS Efq. who was
Born in *Southold* in
yᵉ Year of our Lord
1668 and Departed
this Life *July* yᵉ 29ᵗʰ
Anno Domini 1742

Mʀ IOHN YONGS MINISTER OF THE WORD AND FIRST SETLER
OF THE CHVRCH OF CHRIST IN SOVTHHOVLD ON LONG ISLAND
DECEASED THE 24 OF FEBRVARY IN THE YEARE
OF OVR LORD 167½ AND OF HIS AGE 74
HERE LIES THE MAN WHOSE DOCTRINE LIFE WELL KNOWN
DID SHOW HE SOVGHT CRISTS HONOVR NOT HIS OWN
IN WEAKNES SOWN IN POWER RAISD SHALL BE
BY CHRIST FROM DEATH TO LIFE ETERNALLY

*The original inscription on this stone was recut in 1857 by one of the third &
one of the fourth generations of Rev. John Young's grand children, Dea. Stephen
Youngs, Morristown, N. J., Capt. Selah Youngs, Mattituck, L. I.*

MARY Yᵉ WIFE
OF COLOᴺ JOHN
YOVNGS AGED
59 YEARS
DYED MAY Yᵉ
24 1689

In Memoʳy of
BENJAMIN, Son of
Robert and Mehitabel
Hempfted, who died
Decʳ 18ᵗʰ 1772
aged 3 years & 5 mos.

In Memory of
*Mrs. Mehitabel
Hempfted Relict of
Robert Hempfted Efqʳ.*
who died
July 5ᵗʰ AD. 1791
aged 61 years

IN MEMORY of
MARY the truly pious
Wife of ROBERT
HEMPSTED Efqʳ. who
departed this Life
Janʳʸ the 10ᵗʰ A D 1768
Aged 66 Years 4 Mᵒ
and 27 Days
I have fought a Good fight
I have finished my Courfe
I have kept the faith &c.

In Memory of Betfey Daughter of *Matthew & Abigail C. Wickham* who died July 4th 1787 aged 11 months.
In Memory of *Betfey* Daughter of *Matthew & Abigail C. Wickham* who died March 1ft 1796 aged 4 months.

In
Memory of
Abigail Cleo Wickham,
Wife of
Matthew Wickham
who died Novr 6th
1797, in the 39th year
of her age

HERE LYETH BVRIEᴰ
Yᵉ BODY OF BETHIA
LONGWORTH DAVGHTER
TO THOMAS & DEBORAH
LONGWORTH AGED 15
YEARES 3 Mᵒ 20ᴰ DYED
APRIL Yᵉ 20 1698

In
Memory of
Barnabas T. Terry
Son of
Capt Thomas &
Mrs. Efther Terry
who died
Nov. 30, 1799
aged 2 years
& 5 mo.

IN MEMORY of
Mʳ BENJAMIN BALEY
Deacon of yᵉ Firft Church
of Chrift in Southold
which Office He Suftain'd
about 40 Years & Serv'd
God & His Generation
with great Integrity
He died Novr 10th 1770
Aged 71 Years 1 Mᵒ &
25 Days

IN MEMORY of MARY Daughter of Mʳ BENJAMIN & SUSANNA BAY-LEY died March yᵉ 29th 1731 aged 8 Mᵒ & 19 Days.

IN MEMORY of JONATHAN Son of Mʳ. BENJAMIN & SUSANNA BAY-LEY died July 14th 1739 aged 7 Years 6 Mᵒ & 19 Days.

IN MEMORY of ESTHER Daughter of Mʳ GAMALIEL & ESTHER BAY-LEY died Novr. 11th 1767 aged 2 Mᵒ. Our Lives are ever on the wings And Death is ever nigh, The moment that our Life begins We all begin to die.

IN MEMORY of
SUSANNA the
Wife of Mʳ BENJA-
-MIN BAYLEY who
died Novr yᵉ 1ft
1769 in yᵉ 66th
Year of her Age

Here lyes yᵉ Body of
Mary Petty, Daugᵗʳ
of Mʳ. James & Mʳˢ.
Chriftian Petty
Who Died Sepᵗ 6th
1738 Aged 14 Years
5 Months & 2 Daˢ.

Here lyes yᵉ Body
of James Petty Son
of Mʳ. James & Mʳˢ.
Chriftian Petty
Who Died Novᵇʳ
1ft 1737 Aged 16
Years & 2 Months

HERE LYES Yᵉ BODY
OF Mʳ JAMES
PETTEY AGED 38
YEARS & 3 Mᵒ
DECᴰ DECᴿ Yᵉ
3ᴰ 1726

MARY
CONKLEYN
DECEASED
NOVEMBER 2
1688

In
Memory of
ISRAEL N. H.
HOWELL, who died
July 30th 1800
aged 16 years.

In Memory of
Sylvefter Lefter
Son of Mr Sylvefter
& Mrs. Mary Lefter
who died Febry. 21st. 1780
in his 11th year.

In
Memory of
EUNICE LEDDYARD
formally the wife of
David Goldsmith
who died
Oct. 27, 1795,
Æ 31 years & 10 mo.

NOTES.

WILLIAM WHITEHAIRE, d. 1707, p. 3.   His will, dated Apr. 19, 1707, calls him "weavour," of Southold, "very sick and weak"; to Phebe Corwin, under 18, who lived with him, feather bed, etc.; to beloved wife Deliverance Whitehair all the estate; wife and friend Josha Wells executors. (N. Y. Wills, 7, 495.)

JOSEPH REEVE, d. 1736, p. 4.   Will dated July 19, 1722, and proved June 3, 1736; blacksmith, in "perfect health"; wife Deliverance, sons Joseph, Benjamin, David, Hezekiah, Solomon and William, daus. Abigail, Mary and Hannah; sons Benjamin and William executors. (N. Y. Wills, 12. 514.)

JOHN GOOLDSMITH, d. 1724, p. 5.   Will dated Feb. 25, and proved Mar. 18, 1724-5; yeoman, very sick; wife Mary, sons John, Zaccheus, Jeremiah and Daniel, and daus., one of whom is Mary Wells. (N. Y. Wills, 10, 32.)

SOLMON, p. 5.   In Lib. 1 of N. Y. Wills are recorded the papers connected with the administration of the estate of an early William Solmon, who had married Katherine, the widow of Matthew Sunderland, a seaman, and the owner of lands at Hashamacock.   By her he had four children, and by another wife, Sarah, two others, and died so that his widow Sarah could become the wife of John Conkling before March, 1666, when Conkling was appointed to administer Solmon's estate, and sets forth that he had maintained these "divers young children."   The children who were the heirs of the Hashamacock lands were John, Mary (the oldest daughter), Sarah, Rebecca, Elizabeth and Hannah.

JOHN CONKELYNE, d. 1694, p. 8.   No will appears on record.   A later John, yeoman of Southold, made his will Jan. 15, 1705-6, and it was presented Oct. 14 following, and allowed Jan. 2, 1706-7.   He gave an interest in his lands at Hashamacock to his wife Sarah, and names oldest son John, second son Henry, third Thomas and fourth Joseph, and daus. Sarah, Rachel, Mary and Elizabeth.

BARNABAS HORTON, d. 1680, p. 10.   He made his will May 3, 1680, "findeing sundry Distemps Dayly Growing upon me," naming sons (1) Joseph, (2) Benjamin, (3) Caleb, (4) Joshua, (5) Jonathan, eldest dau. Hannah Trevale, Joseph, the son of dau. Sarah Conckling, third dau. Mary Budd, youngest dau. Mercy Youngs, and wife Mary who shall be sole executrix. (N. Y. Wills, 2, 417.)

RICHARD STEER, d. 1721, p. 14.   He made his will Mar. 29, 1721, being "aged and infirm"; to Joshua Wheeler of New London "a penal obligation," to Elizabeth, wife of Nathaniel Beebe, Elizabeth, wife of Jacob Alley of New London, Mary, dau. of Nathaniel and Elizabeth Beebe, Anna wife of John Tonge, Betty or Elizabeth, dau. of John and Anna Tonge,—these six legatees being "children and grandchildren of my former wife Elizabeth,"—dau. in law Bythia, wife of Isaac Hubbard, and wife Bithye Steer. (N. Y. Wills, 9, 295.)

COL. JOHN YOUNGS, d, 1698, p. 21.   His will of Feb. 20, 1696-7, gave all his lands to his son Thomas Youngs, and to each of his two daus. Deborah Longworth and Martha Gardiner one third of his movable estate.   A small legacy was left to his grandson Daniel Youngs. (N. Y. Wills, 5, 243.)

SOUTHOLD.—EAST MARION.

In Memory of
Mr. James Bailey
Son of *Mr. John* and
Mrs. Charity Bailey,
who died
Augt. 15 AD. 1799
aged 25 years
1 mo. & 1 day.

In
Memory of
HANNAH
daughter of
Mr. Samuel and
Hannah Billard
who died Decr. 16, 1797
aged 4 years
3 mo. & 10 days.

In Memory of
Thomas Moore
Son of
M^r. Thomas &
M^{rs}. Marcy Moore
who died June 28th
1790
Aged 34 years
& 3 months

In
Memory of
SAMUEL
Son of *Mr. Samuel*
& Hannah Billard
who died
Decr. 13, 1797
aged 2 years

In MEMORY of
Capt. Joʃeph Booth,
who departed this life
April 28th AD. 1795
in the 52^d year
of his age.
Tho' Boreas winds and Neptune's waves
Have toʃ'd me to and fro,
By God's decree you plainly ʃee
I'm harbour'd here below.

William Son
of Capt Joʃeph
& M^{rs}.
Elizabeth Booth
Died Decr. 12th
1781
in his 3^d Year

In Memory of
M^r. John Booth
who died Decr. 9th.
AD 1787
in the 55th year
of his Age.

In Memory of
Mr George Booth
who died Feb^{ry} 4th
AD 1774
in the 33^d year
of his Age

In Memory of
Lieu^t. Conftant Booth
who died March 27th
AD : 1774
in the 74th year
of his Age

In Memory of
M^{rs}. Mary Booth
Wife of Lieu^t.
Conftant Booth
who died Augst 31st.
AD : 1769
in the 65th year
of her Age.
*O Grave where is thy
Victory.*

In Memory of
Luther Moore
Son of M^r.
Thomas & M^{rs}.
Marey Moore
who died Feb^{ry}.
24th 1785,
Aged 11 years
& 2 months.

In Memory of
LUTHER MOORE
son of Capt. THOMAS
MOORE, who departed
this Life Augst. the 16th
1764 In the 24th Year
of his Age

In Memory of
Capt. THOMAS MOORE
who departed this Life
May the 10th 1767
In the 62nd Year
of his Age

In Memory of
Jonathan Moore
Son of M^r.
Thomas & M^{rs}.
Marey Moore,
who died Augt 16th
1787
Aged 24 Years
& 3 months.

In Memory
OF
Mrs. Rhoda Youngs
Relict of
Thos. Youngs Efq^r.
who died
January 9th 1798
in the 77th year
of her age

In Memory of
THOMAS YOUNGS Efq.
who departed this life Feb'y 19th
1793 in the 74th Year of his Age
He was the fon of
J. YOUNGS Efq. fon of
Mr ZERUBBABEL YOUNGS,
fon of Col. JOHN YOUNGS,
fon of the Rev. JN'O YOUNGS
the firft from England;
Firft minifter of Southold.

IN MEMORY of
Mary ye Wife of
Jofhua Youngs
Efq^r. who died
April 24th 1765
in ye 78th Year
of her Age

HERE LYES INTERRED
THE BODY OF
JOSHUA YOUNGS Esqr.
WHO DEPARTED THIS
LIFE JUNE THE 22^d
ANNO DOMNI 1755
IN THE 71st YEAR
OF HIS AGE

In memory of an
infant daughter of
Capt. Joshua Youngs
and Mrs. Hannah Yo
ungs. She departed
this life June 12th
1784 aged 12 days
*The young may die
and fo muft you and I.*

In Memory of
William Son of
Thomas Youngs Efq^r.
& Rhoda his Wife
who died Sept^t. 3^d.
AD. 1783
Aged 19 Years
& 44 days

In Memory of M^{rs}
Frances wife of
Mr John Donaghy
& daughter of
M^r. Orange &
M^{rs}. Frances Webb
who died Octr. 15th.
1788
in the 30th year
of her Age.

In Memory of
James. Webb
who died
July 12th 1795
aged 34 years
2 months and
13 days

Thomas Fanning
Son of M^r. David
& M^{rs}. Jane Fanning
died Decr. 11th
1789
Aged 28 Hours

In Memory of
Mr Abraham
King Racket
who died
Septr. 14th 1786
Aged 43 Years

IN
Memory of
Mercy wife of
WILLIAM WIGGINS
who died
Oct. 16, 1793.
Æ. 32.

Sacred to the *MEMORY* of Mrs.
SUSANNA WIGGINS. Wife
of Dr. THOMAS WIGGINS
of Princeton, New Jersey who departe^d
this Life at Sagg Harbour on the 7th of July
AD 1791 aged 58 Years. A lady highly re-
fpected for an acute & firm underftanding, for
her domeftic virtues, fincere & fervent piety.

Sacred to
the *Memory* of
Capt John Wiggins
who departed this
Life Decr. 18th
AD 1767, in the 67th
Year of his Age.

In Memory of
M^{rs}. Dorothy Brown
Wife of M^r.
James Brown :
who died Sep^t. 14th
1785
Aged 62 Years

Sacred to the Memory
of Mrs. Mary
Wiggins, Wife of
Capt. John Wiggins,
who departed
this Life June 2^d
AD 1774 in the 83^d
year of her Age.

In Memory of
M^r. James Brown
who departed this
Life Sep^t. 8th.
1785
Aged 65 Years

In
Memory of
Capt. James Brown
who died
Dec. 29, 1798,
Æ. 42.
Man is born to die

Beneath this duft lies the body of Thomas Brown Son of Capt. James & Mrs.
Rhoda Brown who died Octr. 10th. 1794 aged 4 years 1 month & 6 days. *Life
how fhort! eternity how long.*

In Memory of GEORGE Son of James H. & Deziah Racket, who died June
20, 1797 aged 1 month.

SOUTHOLD.—OLD ORIENT.

On the very narrow neck of land between Orient Harbor and the Sound, just west of the village of Orient, is the old burying-ground of Oyster Pond. It is approached through private grounds, and is hardly a stone's throw from the beach. Here were buried the first settlers of this part of the township. Most of the stones are of imported slate. All of the inscriptions found in 1882 are here printed.*

[Foot-stone: head-stone lost.]
LIEU^T GIDEON
YOUNGS
1 7 4 9

Here lyeth ye Body
of Gideon Youngs
who depar^{td} this life
in ye 61 year of his
age ye 31st day of
Decem^{br} in ye year
1 6 9 9

[EZEKI]EL YOUNGS
SON OF GIDEON
& EUNICE YOUNGS
DEC^D MAY Y^e 13
1727 IN Y^e 3^D YEAR
OF HIS AGE

HERE LYES Y^e BODY
OF WALTER YOUNGS
SON TO GIDEON &
HANNAH YOUNGS DEC^D
MARCH Y^e 1st 1714–15 IN
Y^e 4th YEAR OF HIS AGE

HERE LYES Y^e BODY
OF M^{RS} HANNAH YOUNGS
WIFE OF LIEV^T
GIDEON YOUNGS
DEC^D JUNE 6TH
1 7 3 8
IN Y^e 59th YEAR
OF HER AGE

HERE LYES BURIED
THE BODY OF M^{rs}
DOROTHY YOUNGS
WIFE OF M^r
JONATHAN YOUNGS
WHO DEPARTED THIS
LIFE SEP^T 21^{ft} 1753
IN THE 66th YEAR
OF HER AGE

In Memory of
Rhode ye Daughter of
Lieu^t Gideon Youngs
& Hannah his Wife
who died Aug^{ft} 8th
1765 in ye 57th Year
of her Age

---

* In the preparation of the manuscript of the Orient inscriptions the writer has had the advantage of comparing his own copy of the original stones with one made by Mr. Rufus King and printed in the N. Y. Genealogical and Biographical Record of April, 1875, and, also, with another, made in 1898 by Miss Lucy D. Akerly, the genealogist. And it may be safely asserted that in this presentment no stone has been overlooked, and no name or date need be questioned.

Here lyeth Dorathy yᵉ Daughter of Ionathan & Dorathy Youngˢ who dyed Nouembʳ yᵉ 22 1719 in yᵉ 2 year of her age

HERE LIES Yᵉ BODY OF
PATIANCE TERRY
DAUʳ OF Mʳ
JONATHAN & Mʳˢ
LYDIA TERRY
DIED JULY 18ᵗʰ 1754
AGED 3 YEARS
8 MONTHS & 25 Dˢ

In Memory
of Dorothy yᵉ
Daughter of
Mʳ James Brown
& Dorothy his
wife died Octoʳ
yᵉ 18ᵗʰ 1754 aged
2 Years 9 Mᵒ
& 12 Days

[Foot-stone: the head-stone lost.]
THOMAS
TERRY 1753

In Memory
of Jeremiah fon
of Mʳ Richard &
Mʳˢ Phebe Youngs
he died 1759
aged 13ᵐᵒⁿᵗʰˢ & 14 Dˢ

Here lyes yᵉ Body of
Mʳˢ ESTHER YOUNGS
Wife to Mʳ RICHARD
YOUNGS Who Died
in yᵉ Year 1749 in yᵉ
33ᵈ Year of her Age

HERE LIES BURIED
THE BODY OF Mʳ
JEREMIAH VAIL
WHO DEPARTED THIS
LIFE OCTᴿ 13 1749
AGED 39 YEARS
AND 5 Mᵒ.

Here lyes yᵉ Body
of Mʳ BENJAMIN
TUTHILL; Who
Died Febʳʸ 16ᵗʰ
1748/9 in yᵉ 23ᵈ
Year of his Age

In Memory
of Jonathan
the son of
Jeremiah &
Eliza Vail

[Foot-stone: head-stone lost.]
Mʳˢ SARAH
VAIL 1756

HERE LYES THE
BODY OF Mʳ
JONATHAN TUTHILL
DYED FEBʳʸ 8ᵗʰ 1741/2
IN Yᵉ 50ᵗʰ YEAR
OF HIS AGE

Here lyes yᵉ Body
of Mʳˢ Sufanna
Tuthill, Wife to Mʳ
Jonathan Tuthill
Who Died May 16
1743 in yᵉ 39ᵗʰ Year
of Her Age

HERE LYES Yᵉ BODY
OF CAPᵗ WILLIAM BOOTH
WHO DECᴰ MARCH Yᵉ
11   1 7 2 3
IN Yᵉ 63ᴰ YEAR

Here lyes yᵉ Body
of Mʳˢ Hannah
Booth, wife to Capᵗ
William Booth
Who departed this
Life Decᵇʳ 22ᵈ AD. 1742
in yᵉ 76ᵗʰ Year of her Age

GEORGE SON OF
WILLIAM &
HANNAH BOOTH
DIED IN Yᵉ 17 YEAR
OF HIS AGE NOVʳ
1 7 1 3

HERE LYETH
WILLIAM Y^e SON OF
WILLIAM BOOTH
& OF HANNAH
HIS WIFE WHO DEC
IN Y^e 22^D YEAR
OF HIS AGE IVLY
Y^e 22^D 1712

Here lyeth
the Body of
Samuel King
who died in
the 89th Year
of his age
Novem^{br} ye 29th
1 7 2 1

HERE LYETH Y^e BODY
OF JONATHAN BROWN
WHO DEPARTED THIS
LIFE AVGVST Y^e 19
1710 IN Y^e 57
YEAR OF HIS AGE

Here lyeth the
body of Hannah
the wife of Henry
Tuthill who deceast
in ye 24th year of
her age Decemb^r
the first 1 7 1 5

Here lieth Interred
the Body of Richard
King, who died May
ye 20th 1735 in ye 24th
year of his age.
As you pafs by behold and see
As I am now so muft you be
Make fure of Chrift to be your Friend
And peace fhall be your Latter End

Here lieth Bezaleel ye son
of William & Bathfhua
King died April ye 24 1735
In ye 9th year of his age.
In the cold earth behold I lie
Who once was Living as you be
Theirs none so young but they may Die
Prepare for Death and Follow me.

[BA]THSHUA KING
Beneath this little Stone here lies
The Wife of William King
And tho' fhe's dead to Mortal Eyes
She will Revive again.
Liv'd four and Fifty Years a Wife
Dy'd in her Seventy Seven
Has now laid down her Mortal Life
In hopes to live in Heaven,
May ye 7th A D 1764

HERE LIES THE BODY OF
PAUL KING SON OF M^r
WILLIAM & Mⁿ BATHSHUA
KING DEC^D NOV^R 26th
1750 IN Y^e 20th
YEAR OF HIS AGE
Youth caft an eye as you pass by
And view the ground whare now I [lie]
Prepare for Death while you are y[oung]
Who knows how soon your [turn may come].

IN MEMORY of
Sufannah ye Wife of
Robert Sheffield &
Daughter of William
& Bathfhua King who
died May 1^{ft} 1766 in
the 43^d Year of her Age

IN MEMORY of
Sufannah Daughter ^{of}
Robert & Sufannah
Sheffield who
died May 1^{ft} 1766
In ye 16th Year
of her Age

Here lieth
David ye Son
of David &
Hannah King
died Sepr ye 7
1729 in ye 13th
Year of his age

31

Here lieth yᵉ
Body of Hannah yᵉ
wife of David King
died Janʳʸ yᵉ 11ᵗʰ 1728-9
in yᵉ 33ᵈ Year of her age
Her turn is come Next May be thine
Prepare for it whilſt Thou haſt time
And that Thou Mayeſt prepared be
Live unto him that died for Thee

Robert yᵉ
Son of
Robert &
Sufanna
Sheffield
died Auguſt
yᵉ 7ᵗʰ 1753
Aged 19 Mᵒ

Here Lyes Elisabeth
Once Samuel Beebees wife
Who once was made a living foul
But's now depriv'd of life
yet firmly
Did believe
That at her Lord's return
Shee fhould be made a living foul
In his own fhap and form
Liv'd four and thirty years a Wife
Was Aged fifty feven
Has now lay'd down her mortal foul
In hope to live in Heaven
Iune the 10ᵗʰ 1716

Here lyeth the
Body of Sarah
the Wife of Iohn
Paine who dyed
in the 76 year
of her age
Septemᵇʳ yᵉ 3ᵈ 1716

Here lyeth
the Body of
Bezᵉlel King
who died in
the 22 Year
of his age Feb
yᵉ 12ᵗʰ 1725

HERE LYES Yᵉ BODY
OF Mʳˢ SUSANNA KING
WHO DIED MAY
THE 10ᵗʰ 1741
IN Yᵉ 63ᴅ YEAR
OF HER AGE

Here lyeth the
Body of Abigall
the Wife of William
King who dyed in
the 50ᵗʰ year of
her age May
the 27ᵗʰ 1716

Here lyeth
yᵉ body of Martha
yᵉ wife of charles
glouer who dep
arted this life may
yᵉ 5ᵗʰ in yᵉ yeare of
of our lord christ
1713 & in yᵉ 36ᵗʰ
year of her age

HERE
LYETH THE
BODY OF MARY
BROWN Yᵉ WIFE
OF SAMVEL
BROWN WHO
DIED MAY 31
1711 IN THE
20ᵗʰ YEAR OF
HER AGE

HERE LYES Yᵉ
BODY OF Mʳ
SAMUEL KING JUNʳ
DECᴰ MAY Yᵉ 6ᵗʰ
1 7 2 5
IN Yᵉ 51ˢᵗ YEAR
OF HIS AGE

BODY
[broken off] IFE
KING
ARTᴰ THIS
GUST Yᵉ 17
IN Yᵉ 32ᵗʰ
YEAR OF HER AGE

32

IN MEMORY of
MARY yᵉ wife of
JOHN WIGGINS
Junʳ died April
yᵉ 9ᵗʰ 1766 in yᵉ
40ᵗʰ year of her
Age;

Here lyeth the
Body of Edward
Iohnson who
dyed in the 69ᵗʰ
year of his age
octobʳ yᵉ 21ˢᵗ 1717

HERE LIES Yᵉ BODY OF
ABSALOM KING
SON OF ENSIGN
JOHN KING
& Mʳˢ MARY HIS WIFE
DIED OCTʳ 15ᵗʰ
1 7 5 2
IN THE 20ᵗʰ YEAR
OF HIS AGE

HERE LIES INTERR'D
Yᵉ BODY OF INSIGN
JOHN KING
WHO DEPARTED THIS
LIFE JUNE 28ᵗʰ
1 7 5 3
IN THE 54ᵗʰ YEAR
OF HIS AGE

HERE LYES BURIED
THE BODY OF
CAPᵗ JOHN KING
WHO DIED JANʳʸ
Yᵉ 19ᵗʰ 1741/2
IN Yᵉ 64ᵗʰ YEAR
OF HIS AGE

HERE LIES THE BODY OF
Mʳˢ KATHARINE KING
THE WIFE OF CAPᵗ
JOHN KING
WHO DEPARTED THIS
LIFE JULY THE 21ˢᵗ
1 7 5 2
AGED 68 YEARS

HERE LYES BURIED Yᵉ
BODY OF Mʳ. CHRISTOPHER
BROWN SON TO CAPᵀ RICHARD
& ANNA BROWN AGED 25 YEARS
& 2 Mᵒ DECᴰ AUGᵀ Yᵉ 25ᵗʰ
1 7 3 9

Here lyes Buried
yᵉ Body of Doctʳ
PETER BROWN ;
Who departed this Life
June yᵉ 4ᵗʰ A D 1747 In
yᵉ 28ᵗʰ Year of his Age

HERE LYES BURIED
THE BODY OF
ANNA BROWN
DAUʳ OF Mʳ
RICHARD & Mʳˢ
HANNAH BROWN
DIED AUGᵗ 13ᵗʰ 1753
IN THE 8ᵗʰ YEAR
OF HER AGE

Here lieth yᵉ
Body of John Hopkins
died July yᵉ 22
1727 in yᵉ 22
Year of his age

Here lyes yᵉ body of
William Hopkins the
husband of Rebecca
Hopkins who departed
this life June yᵉ 26ᵗʰ
1 7 1 8

GENEALOGICAL NOTES ON OLD ORIENT EPITAPHS.

By Miss Lucy D. Akerly, of Newburgh, N. Y.

Lieut. Gideon[4] Youngs, d. 1749, p. 28. He was son of Gideon[3] (d. 1699) and Sarah, and was about 76 at his death in 1749. He used a lion *sejant* seal.

Gideon[3] Youngs, d. 1699, p. 28. He was son of Capt. Joseph[2] and Margaret, nephew of Rev. John[2] Youngs, and through either father or mother, grandson of Rev. Christopher[1] Youngs, vicar of Reydon and Southwold, co. Suffolk, England.

Ezekiel[6] Youngs, d. 1727, p. 28. He was son of Gideon[5] (*Lieut. Gideon[4]*) by his first wife Eunice Petty.

Dorothy Youngs, d. 1753, p. 28. She was daughter of Ensign Richard[3] Brown (*Lieut. Richard[2]*), b. April 3, 1688, mar. 1708–9 Jonathan[4] Youngs.

Dorothy Youngs, d. 1719, p. 28. She was daughter of Jonathan,[4] who was elder brother of Lieut. Gideon[4] Youngs.

Dorothy Brown, d. 1754, p. 29. Her mother, Dorothy, is supposed to have been a dau. of Joseph and Dorothy (Tuthill) Brown.

Patience Terry, d. 1754, p. 29. She was a daughter of Jonathan[4] (*Thomas,[3] Thomas,[2] Thomas[1]*) by wife Lydia Tuthill (*Daniel,[4] John,[3] Henry,[2] Henry[1]*).

Thomas Terry, d. 1753, p. 29. Brother of the last, d. Nov. 12, 1753, in his 14th year.

Esther Youngs, d. 1749, p. 29. Richard[5] Youngs, her husband (and the father of Jeremiah,[6] d. 1759) was son of Jonathan[4] and Dorothy (Brown) Youngs. His first wife was Esther (Warren?). His will dated May 30, 1765 (*vide* N. Y. co. Wills, Lib. 25, p. 187), names wife Phebe, sons Richard, Warren, Daniel and Henry, and daughters Esther and Susanna not yet eighteen.

Jeremiah[4] Vail, d. 1749, p. 29. He was probably son of Jeremiah,[3] and mar. Apr. 6, 1732, Elizabeth Yonges (*Joshua, Zerubabel?, Col. John, Rev. John*). Jeremiah[1] Vail was at Salem 1639, and afterwards at Gardiner's Island, East Hampton and Southold; his first wife, mother of Jeremiah,[2] is unknown (he mar. (2) widow Mary Payne, and (3) Joyce ———). Jeremiah[2] mar. Ann widow of Benjamin Moore, and was father of Jeremiah.[3]

Benjamin Tuthill, d. 1748–9, p. 29. He was doubtless son of Jonathan[5] Tuthill (d. 1741–2) (*Henry,[4] John,[3] Henry,[2] Henry[1]*), who mar. Feb. 23, 1723, Susanna (d. 1743), dau. of Benjamin and Patience (Sylvester) L'Hommedieu, grand dau. of Capt. Nathaniel Sylvester of Shelter Island, and great grand dau. of Thomas Brinley, Esq. of Staffordshire, England, auditor to K. Charles 1.

Capt. William Booth, d. 1723, p. 29. He mar. 1688, Hannah (d. 1742) King (*Samuel,[2] William[1]*), b. Jan. 26, 1666; of their issue, William (d. 1712) was b. May 25, 1689, and George (d. 1713) was b. Apr. 28, 1696. *Vide* Booth Genealogy for earlier data of the family.

Jonathan Brown, d. 1710, p. 30. He was doubtless Jonathan, the second son of Lieut. Richard[2] Brown. He mar. Elizabeth, dau. of Capt. Nathaniel Sylvester of Shelter Island.

Samuel King, d. 1721, p. 30. He was a son of William and Dorothy (Hayne?) King of Salem, mar. Oct. 10, 1660, Frances, dau. of William and Clemence Ludlam of Matlock, England, and Southampton, N. Y., who died Jan. 14, 1692, aged about 53 yrs.*

Hannah Tuthill, d. 1715, p. 30. Her identity is in dispute. Keith, in his *Ancestry of Benjamin Harrison*, surmises that her surname was Crouch. Griffin says she was a dau. of Samuel[5] Beebe of Plum Island, but a deed of Beebe's shows that his dau. Hannah mar. David King. The late Charles B. Moore stated that her name was Booth, and a careful study of the subject by the present writer would seem to render this position highly probable. If so, she was probably that dau. of Capt. William[2] and Hannah (King) Booth (*see ante*)

[*The King data comprised in these Notes are obtained through the courtesy of Mr. Rufus King of Yonkers. For a complete presentation of the subject reference may be had to the King Charts published by him in 1887 and 1891.]

who was born Feb. 22, 1691. Hannah Tuthill was the great grandmother of Anna Symmes, the wife of President William Henry Harrison.

RICHARD KING, d. 1735, p. 30. He was b. Nov. 5, 1711, son of William[4] and Bathshua (Beebe) King.

BEZALEEL KING, d. 1735, p. 30. Brother of the last, b. Mar. 31, 1727.

BATHSHUA KING, d. 1764, p. 30. She was b. May 16, 1688, dau. of Samuel and Elizabeth (Rogers) Beebe of Plum Island. Her issue by William[4] King, b. Feb. 14, 1677-8 (*William,*[3] *Samuel,*[2] *William*[1]), were:—William[5] (mar. Elizabeth Beebe), Richard, Hannah (mar. Richard Baxter), James, Bathsheba, Susanna (mar. Robert Sheffield), Bezaleel and Paul.

PAUL KING, d. 1750, p. 30. He was b. May 2, 1731, son of above Bathshua.

SUSANNA SHEFFIELD, d. 1766, p. 30. She was b. May 29, 1723, mar. June 22, 1749. Four children born to Robert and Susannah Sheffield are recorded in Lib. E. Southold Records, of whom SUSANNAH (d. 1766) was b. Dec. 7, 1750, and ROBERT (d. 1753), was b. June 21, 1752.

HANNAH KING, d. 1728-9, p. 31. She was b. Apr. 5, 1695, dau. of Samuel and Elizabeth (Rogers) Beebe, mar. Sept. 5, 1715. Her husband David[4] King (*William,*[3] *Samuel,*[2] *William*[1]), b. Oct. 22, 1693, was drowned Sept. 26, 1749, having mar. 1731 (2) Deborah the dau. of William[3] (Samuel,[2] Charles[1]) Glover.

ELIZABETH BEEBEE, d. 1716, p. 31. She was b. Apr. 15, 1658, dau. of James Rogers of Stratford, Milford and New London, Conn., for whom May Flower ancestry, though often claimed, remains unproved. She mar. Feb. 9, 1682, Samuel[5] Beebe of Plum Is., popularly known as "King" Beebe, who d. July, 1742. He was son, not of Joseph, as asserted by Griffin, but of Samuel[4] of New London, who mar. (1) Agnes[2] Keeney (William[1]), probably the mother of all his children, and (2) her sister Mary, b. 1640. Samuel[4] was son of John[3] Beebe, who d. May 18, 1650, on the passage to America, sometime of Broughton, Northamptonshire, son of John[2] (and Alice), son of Alexander[1] and Elizabeth, all of Great Addington, Northamptonshire.

SARAH PAINE, d. 1716, p. 31. Her husband John Paine is not identified. Thomas Payne, the emigrant, died in Salem about 1650, leaving widow Elizabeth (possibly a dau. of Henry Tuthill of Tharston, co. Norfolk, England) who came to Southold with several of their children.

BEZELEL KING, d. 1725, p. 31. He was b. Jan. 23, 1703-4, son of William and Abigail.(Brown) King.

ABIGALL KING, d. 1716, p. 31. She was dau. of Lieut. Richard and Hannah (King) Brown, and mar. Jan. 17, 1686-7, her first cousin William[3] (*Samuel,*[2] *William*[1]) King. who was b. Jan. 10, 1661-2, and d. May 12, 1740, having mar. (2) Jan. 20, 1716, SUSANNA Crook (d. 1741).

MARTHA GLOVER, d. 1713, p. 31. Charles Glover, her husband, was probably son of Lieut. Samuel[2] (*Charles*[1]) Glover, and his wife Sarah[2] (*Thomas*[1]) Moore, as the dates hardly admit of his having been the son of Samuel[3] as stated in a modern note in the Southold Town Records. The emigrant, Charles[1] Glover, a shipwright, was at Salem, Mass., in 1632, and died at Southold in Jan., 1665. His first wife died in March, 1648, the mother of Mary,[2] wife of John Corwin, Elizabeth,[2] wife of Geoffrey Jones, and Lieut. Samuel.[2] His second wife was divorced, and he mar. (3) Esther Saunders, widow, probably dau. of John and Ann Rolfe of Southampton, L. I., and Newbury, Mass.

MARY BROWN, d. 1711, p. 31. She was doubtless first wife of Samuel[4] (*Ensign Richard,*[2] *Lieut. Richard,*[2] *Richard*[1]?), who was b. Mar. 21, 1686, and d. Apr. 30, 1725. He doubtless was the same who mar. (2) Jan. 14, 1712-13, Rebecca, dau. of Samuel[5] and Elizabeth (Rogers) Beebe, b. Mar. 25, 1690.

SAMUEL KING, d. 1725, p. 31. He was b. 23 (1) 1675, son of Samuel[2] (*William*[1]). He mar. Jan. 1, 1697, Hannah, erroneously supposed to have been a dau. of Jonathan Havens.

The mutilated inscription on the next stone may, with a good deal of confidence, be restored thus:—

[HERE LYES Y^e] BODY [OF M^rs]
HANNAH KING [W]IFE [OF M^r]
[SAMUEL] KING [JUN^r]
[WHO DEP]ART^D THIS [LIFE]
[AU]GUST Y^e 17, [1712]
IN Y^e 39th
YEAR OF HER AGE

MARY WIGGINS, d. 1766, p. 32. She was b. Jan. 27, 1726, dau. of Ensign John[4] King (Samuel,[3] Samuel,[2] William[1]) by his wife Mary (Corey). She mar. (1) May, 1746, Dr. Peter Brown, (2) Mar. 6, 1754, John Wiggins; issue by both husbands.

EDWARD JOHNSON, d. 1717, p. 32. One Mr. Edward Johnson of New London bought land at Orient in 1718. He was described in 1714 as a shipwright, and was a married man at the time. Possibly the Edward buried here was a relative of Lot Johnson of Southold, of William Johnson who mar. Elizabeth[3] Tuthill (Henry,[2] Henry[1]), or " of the wife of John Tooker of Southold and Brookhaven, whose first wife was probably Mary Johnson from Hingham, England."

ABSALOM KING, d. 1752, p. 32. He was b. Oct. 5, 1733, son of Ensign John[4] and Mary (Corey) King.

ENSIGN JOHN KING, d. 1753, p. 32. He was b. July 15, 1699, son of Samuel[3] (Samuel,[2] William[1]), and mar. June 25, 1724, Mary Corey, probably dau. of Abraham[3] (Abraham,[2] John[1]), b. Jan. 11, 1707. Her surname has been sometimes erroneously given as Brown.

CAPT. JOHN[3] KING, d. 1741-2, p. 32. He was b. Jan. 26, 1677. (Samuel,[2] William[1]), mar. Aug. 22, 1704, KATHARINE (d. 1752) Osborne, b. Aug. 21, 1684. His will (N. Y. co. Lib. 14, p. 269) names among other children, his daughters Mary Booth and Elizabeth Hopkins. Of these, Mary,[4] b. July 22, 1705, and Oct. 1726, her 1st cousin, Lieut. Constant[3] (Capt. William[2] by wife Hannah[3] (King)) Booth, b. Jan. 8, 1701; and Elizabeth,[4] mar. Dec. 26, 1734, Abijah, son of William and Rebecca Hopkins of Shelter Island, William being buried at Orient, as are Capt. William and Hannah Booth.

CHRISTOPHER BROWN, d. 1739, p. 32. He was b. June 29, 1714, son of Capt. Richard[4] and Anna (Youngs) Brown.

PETER BROWN, d. 1747, p. 32. He was b. Sept. 11, 1719, brother of the last, and grandson of Ensign Richard[3] and Dorothy (King) Brown, and great grandson of Lieut. Richard[2] and Hannah (King) Brown. Apparently Richard[2] was a son of Richard,[1] who d. Oct. 16, 1655, according to Moore's Indexes.

ANNA BROWN, d. 1753, p. 32. Doubtless the dau. of Richard[5] Brown (brother of Christopher and Peter above) and his wife Hannah (Hawk), b. Apr. 30, 1745.

JOHN HOPKINS, d. 1727, p. 32. He was son of William,[3] b. 1660 (Giles,[2] Stephen[1] of the Mayflower).

WILLIAM HOPKINS, d. 1718, p. 32. Rebecca (Havens?), wife of William, d. Apr. 23, 1746. His will mentions eight children, but six of whom are known by name, viz: William, Eferam, Hannah, Samuel, John, and Abijah, who mar. Elizabeth, dau. of Capt. John[3] King, in 1734.

EUNICE YOUNGS, d. 1725. A mutilated stone contains enough of an inscription to enable us, with the help of the town records, to construct the following :—

Here lyes ye Body
of Eunice Youngs
ye Wife of Gideon
Youngs Junr who died
May ye 8 1715
In ye 24 year
of her Age.

Gideon[5] Youngs (Lieut. Gideon,[4] Gideon,[3] Capt. Joseph,[2] Rev. Christopher[1]?) b. Dec. 7, 1698, d. Dec. 25, 1780, mar. (1) Eunice Petty, (2) Rachel Rackett, b. Sep. 12, 1708, d. Nov. 23, 1787.

MICHAL TUTHILL, the fragment of whose stone remains, was dau. of Gideon[5] and Rachel (Rackett) Youngs, b. Sep. 9, 1734, d. Feb. 26, 1756, O.S., mar. Aug. 7, 1755, N.S., Nathaniel[6] Tuthill (Nathaniel,[5] Daniel,[4] John,[3] Henry,[2] Henry[1]).

SOUTHOLD.—ORIENT VILLAGE.

The following inscriptions are from stones in a small burial-ground on the south side of the main road in the village of Orient. The slabs are of sand stone from the Connecticut quarries across the Sound, and only six bearing dates earlier than 1800 were standing in 1882. Asa King and his wife Mary conveyed this land by deed, dated August 26, 1790, to Christopher Brown, and others, for burial purposes.

In Memory of
Mr. Benjamin King,
who departed this Life
Sepr. 23^d 1793,
Aged 71 years
& 8 Months.

Come friends & children who ſurvive my fall
Drop a ſad tear & hear your Saviour's call
Death ſoon will lay you as you ſee me lie
Prepare to meet your God before you die.

Here lies the body
of M^r. *Asa King,*
who departed
this life
Septr. 16th AD 1796,
aged 72 years.
My friends and all who
come to view my grave
Remember you this bed
of clay muſt have.

In Memory of
PATIENCE
Daugh^r. of Amon
& Sibbil Taber,
who died Jan. 16th
1799 in the 12th
year of her age.
Reader you muſt
ſoon turn to duſt.

In Memory of
M^{rs}. Elizabeth King,
wife of
M^r. Benjn. King,
who departed this Life
June 23^d 1794
Aged 71 years
& 5 Months.

Children ſtop here ſee where your parents lie
And think how ſoon you may be call'd to die
We once were living, now we both are dead
And in this silent grave our bodies laid.

Thomas Vincent
Tuthill, Son of
Capt. Rufus &
Mary Tuthill;
died March 14th
1790. Aged 16 Years.
" *Up to the Courts
where Angels dwell,
It mounts triumphant
there.*"

In Memory of Mifs
Cynthia, Daughter of
Capt. Rufus & M^{rs}.
Mary Tuthill, who
died Jan^{ry} 20th 1791;
in the 19th Year
of her Age.

date

*Ye blooming youth who read my
And drop the friendly tears,
Remember, you may fhare
my fate,
And DIE in early years.*

KING NOTE.

THE King family, so largely represented in the burial-grounds of Southold, is descended from William King, who sailed from Weymouth, England, in March 1635-6, accompanied by his wife Dorothy, and five children, and settled at Salem, Massachusetts. The father died in Salem about 1650, intestate, and his estate was settled by the widow, and oldest son, William.

Some time later, the second son, Samuel, was found at Southold, where he was ultimately joined by his mother, Dorothy, and where she was living certainly as late as in 1684. The identity of mother and son with the Salem people is fully established. Samuel[2] married Abigail, the daughter of William Ludlam. He died in Southold, Nov. 29, 1721, aged 88. Three sons, all of Southold, outlived him, William,[3] Samuel[3] and John[3], whose descendants liberally populated the eastern end of Long Island in both male and female lines.

Capt. John[3] King, the youngest son of Samuel,[2] b. 1678, d. Jan. 19, 1741-2, was the father of that Benjamin (b. June 24, 1722) who with his wife Elizabeth are buried in the Orient Village ground.

Mr. Rufus[8] King, of Yonkers, N.Y., to whose genealogical labors at home and abroad a large number of Kings are indebted for their family history, is a descendant of Capt. John's older brother, Samuel,[3] of Southold, through John,[4] John,[5] Rufus[6] and Rufus-Sylvester,[7] the last of Southold and of New York City.

SOUTHOLD ESTATES IN NEW YORK SURROGATE'S OFFICE-

DAVID CARWITHY (Lib. 1, 8), will dated Aug. 30, 1665, names son Caleb, and Caleb's dau. Martha, dau. Elizabeth Crowner, son David, dau. Sarah Curtis, who is executrix; will submitted for proof Nov., 1665.

PHILEMON DICKERSON (Lib. 1, 101), will (not on record here) proved at South-old June, 1672; administration granted to Mary, the widow, Oct. 28, 1672.

JOHN ELTON (Lib. 1, 113), will dated April 19, 1675, names wife, Isaac Oven-ton, his sister's son, and dau.-in-law, Anna Nicolls; recorded June 25, 1675.

WILLIAM PURRIER (Lib. 1, 141), will dated Dec. 13, 1671, names grandson James Reeve, the son of eldest dau. Mary Reeve, Sarah Mapes and Martha Osman, testator's "two youngest" daus., Isaac Reeve, grandchild Mary Windes, and Thomas Terrill, husband of grand-dau. Mary Reeve; will admitted May 13, 1676.

WILLIAM SOLMON (Lib. 1, 17), see *ante* p. 24, Notes.

THOMAS TERRY (Lib. 1, 99), will dated Nov. 26, 1671, names wife, son Daniel, son Thomas, dau. Elizabeth Terry, dau. Ruth Terry, dau. Mary Reeves; will presented June 5, 1672.

RICHARD TERRY (Lib. 1, 137), will without date, names wife Abigail, son Gershom, son Samuel, brother Thomas Terry, dau. Abigail (probably wife of Thomas Rider), son Nathaniel, son Richard, and son John; letters granted to widow May 13, 1676.

BARNABAS HORTON (Lib. 1, 417), see *ante* p. 24, Notes.

JOHN BUDD (Lib. 3, 7), will of Oct. 27, 1684, names wife Mary, oldest son John, younget son Joseph, dau. Mary wife of Christopher Youngs, dau. Hannah wife of Jonathan Hart, dau. Anna Budd, dau. Sarah Budd; will proved Nov. 12, 1684; testator d. Nov. 5, 1684.

JOHN YOUNGS (Lib. 3, 16), widow Mary appointed to administer Jan. 27, 1685.

JOHN YOUNGS (Lib. 5, 243), see *ante* p. 24, Notes.

THOMAS BOOTH (Lib. 7, 376), administration to his son Thomas Booth, Feb. 11, 1706.

JONAH BOWER (Lib. 7, 560), will of May 9, 1709, names eldest son Daniel, brother Isaac Bower, son Jonah, son Stephen, son Ebenezer, two daus. Mehi-tabel Bower and Hannah Bower, son Ezekiel a minor and incompetent, and wife Ruth; proved Nov. 17, 1709.

JOHN CONKLING (Lib. 7, 8), see *ante* p. 24, Notes.

SIMON GROVER (Lib. 7, 371), will of Oct. 2, 1699, names wife Elizabeth, dau. Elizabeth Horton, dau. Mary Youngs, dau. Martha Moore; proved Feb. 8, 1706, when letters were granted to relict Elizabeth.

ZACCHEUS GOLDSMITH (Lib. 7, 379), will of Jan. 17, 1706, names wife Mary (should she "happen to be with child"), bro. Richard Goldsmith, bro. Thomas Goldsmith, bro. John Goldsmith, and sister Mary Goldsmith; proved Jan. 22, 1706.

JONATHAN HORTON (Lib. 7, 495), will of Feb. 21, 1706-7, names son Jonathan, son William, youngest son James, grandson Jonathan the son of deceased son Caleb, dau. Bethiah wife of Henry Tuthill, dau. Mehitable wife of Daniel Tuthill, dau. (widow) Mary Goldsmith, dau. Abigail Horton, dau. Patience Horton, gr. dau. Mehitable the dau. of deceased son Barnabas, and wife Be-thiah; proved June 2, 1708.

RICHARD HOWELL (Lib. 7, 568), will of Aug. 24, 1709, names wife Elizabeth, son John, son David, son Richard, son Jonathan, son Isaac, son Jacob, and dau. Dorothy Reeve; proved Jan 1, 1709-10.

JAMES PETTY (Lib. 7, 337), letters of administration granted to his widow Experience, Oct. 14, 1706.

WILLIAM WHITEHAIRE (Lib. 7, 495), see *ante* p. 24, Notes.

WALTER BROWNE (Lib. 8, 48), letters of administration to his widow Jane, May 1, 1711.

JOHN REEVE (Lib. 8, 342), will of Dec. 15, 1712, weaver, names wife Martha, son John, son Elisha, son Walter, dau. Hannah the wife of Gideon Youngs, sons Nathan and Samuel, son Jonathan, two daus. Abigail and Martha; proved April 2, 1713.

SYMON RAMSEY (Lib. 9, 482), will of March 29, 1719, names son Symon, wife Mary, dau. Rachel, minor dau. Sarah, Mary the wife of Daniel Curwin, and Hannah the wife of Theophilus Curwin; proved Sept. 26, 1723.

RICHARD STEER (Lib. 9, 295), see *ante* p. 24, Notes.

JOHN GOLDSMITH (Lib. 10, 32), see *ante* p. 24, Notes.

DAVID PARSHELL (Lib. 10, 157), will of Jan. 24, 1726, names eldest son David, youngest son Jonathan, bro. Israel Parshall; minor and unmr. daus. (not named); proved March 16, 1725-6.

GERSHOM TERRY, Jr. (Lib. 10, 162), will of Feb. 21, 1724-5, names wife Mary, second son David, dau. Mary Terry under 18, eldest son Gershom, brother Richard Terry; proved Nov. 26, 1726.

JEREMIAH VAILL (Lib. 10, 381), will of Jan. 2, 1722-3, names wife Anna, son Thomas, eldest son Jeremiah, dau. Mary Goldsmith, dau. Martha Horton; proved Jan. 31, 1726-7.

JOSEPH BUDD (Lib. 11, 218), died intestate, administration Feb. 2, 1731, to his brother Joshua.

JOSEPH KING (Lib. 11, 496), will of Nov. 2, 1732, joyner, names wife Mary then without issue, "all my brothers and sisters," "honored father and mother," brother Ellick, brother Constant Booth; proved Dec. 1, 1732.

JAMES REEVE (Lib. 11, 387), will of Jan. 15, 1731-2, names wife Deborah, first son James, kinswoman Deborah wife of David Howell, Jr., grandson Joshua Wells, son Daniel Reeve, son-in-law Nathaniel Warner; proved Aug. 24, 1732.

WILLIAM BROWNE (Lib. 12, 1), will of March 4, 1725-6, names wife Katherine, eldest son William, son Walter, son Silvanus, son David, son Elijah, son Thomas; proved Feb. 26, 1732.

JOHN BRADDICK (Lib. 12, 215), mariner, will of Sept. 6, 1733, names wife Mary, son John, dau. Mary, partner Thomas Sandiforth (Sandford?), five youngest children, viz. Alce, Elizabeth, David, Peter and Abigail; proved Sept. 6, 1734.

DAVID GARDINER (Lib. 12, 52), will of Oct. 21, 1732, names wife, son David, dau. Mary Parshall, dau. Bethiah Wells, dau. Patience Gardiner; proved June 18, 1733.

JACOB HOWELL (Lib. 12, 3), intestate, administration granted March 9, 1732, to David Howell, brother, and Margaret, the widow.

JOHN HOWELL (Lib. 12, 138), will of Dec. 14, 1733, names wife Hannah, son John by former wife Margaret, son Jonathan by wife Hannah, three daus. Eunice, Jemimah and Esther; proved Feb. 12, 1733-4.

JOSEPH REEVE (Lib. 12, 487), see p. 24, Notes.

JOHN SHERRIL (Lib. 12, 291), intestate, administration granted April 12, 1735, "to Recompense Sherril and Thomas Brown, brothers of" deceased.

JOHN TERRY (Lib. 12, 136), will of June 6, 1728, names wife Hannah, three daus. Sarah, Hannah and Abigail, son John, son Samuel, son Richard, son Robert; proved Sept. 3, 1733.

JOSEPH WICKHAM (Lib. 12, 195), will of April 20, 1734, calls himself "Esq.," names son Joseph, son William, son Benjamin, dau. Elizabeth Gardiner, gr. dau. Elizabeth Stoder, son Samuel and son Jonathan; proved Aug. 17, 1734.

JOSIAH YOUNGS (Lib. 12, 8), will of June 17, 1728, names son Josiah, dau. Bethiah Hollioak, and her husband Noah Holioak, wife Experience; proved March 17, 1732.

SAMUEL CROOKE (Lib. 13, 6), intestate, administration to son Samuel June 24, 1736.

JOSEPH GOLDSMITH (Lib. 13, 7), will of May 22, 1734, blacksmith, names son Joshua, dau. Rebeckah Goldsmith, son Josias, "daughters Mary Dickeson & Sary wife & Hannah Case & Elizabeth Corwin" [so in the official copy]; proved June 3, 1736.

JAMES LANDON (Lib. 13, 314), will of Sept. 11, 1738, cordwainer, names son James who is to have house and lands in Litchfield, Ct., minor son John, son Joseph, son Daniel, son David, son Nathan, daus. Mary, Rachel, Lydia and Anne, wife Mary, brother John Vail; proved March 26, 1738-9.

THOMAS REEVES (Lib. 13, 323), will of Feb. 11, 1735-6, blacksmith, names eldest son Abner, wife Mary; proved June 5, 1739.

THOMAS TERRY (Lib. 13, 433), will of Nov. 7, 1739, names wife Mehitabel, eldest dau. Ruth under 21, son Thomas, youngest dau. Mehitabel under 18, and brother Jonathan Terry; proved March 22, 1739-40.

WAITE YOUNGS (Lib. 13, 169), intestate, administration to John Youngs Dec. 1736.

JOSEPH CONKLYNE (Lib. 13, 435), will of Aug. 20, 1739, names wife Lydia, n Joseph, dau. Abigail Conkline, dau. Desire Conkline under 21, son Benjamin ider 21; proved Feb. 6, 1739-40.

THOMAS DICKERSON (Lib. 13, 438), will of May 27, 1725, names eldest son homas, second son Daniel, third son, Joshua, fourth son Joseph, wife Abigail, us. Abigail and Elizabeth, brother John Dickerson; executors declining to rve, son Daniel granted letters April 10, 1739.

JONATHAN BRADLEY (Lib. 13, 442), will of July 31, 1739, names sons Peter id Grant Bradley, daus. Mary, Mehittable, Hannah and Martha, brother-in- w Lieut. Constant Booth, and brother Daniel Tuthill; proved Nov. 23, 1739.

BENJAMIN YOUNGS (Lib. 14, 268), intestate, administration to Ebenezer rime, John Ledyard and Robert Hempstead, sons-in-law of deceased, Aug. 6, '42.

JACOB ALDDRICH (Lib. 16, 116), will of Oct. 21, 1746, names wife Bethiah, uldridg, sons. Peter, Gershom, Jacob, Daniel and Stephen; proved Nov. 10, 146.

SHELTER ISLAND.

SHELTER ISLAND, situated in the waterway between the two eastern peninsulas of Long Island, and equidistant from the towns of Southold and Easthampton, is of very irregular shape, with an extreme length in one direction of about six miles, and in the other of about four. Formerly belonging to Southold, in 1730 it was incorporated as a separate township. The Sylvesters were, for a time, its sole owners, parting with portions in 1695 to William Nicholl and George Havens.

The burial ground from which these inscriptions were taken is near the geographical centre of the island. It is in two parts, the larger being on the south side of the road, and opposite the Presbyterian church edifice, while the smaller is in the rear of that building, and on the north side of the road. All epitaphs of date prior to 1800, which were found there in August, 1881, are here printed. A small private ground of the Nicoll Family, about three miles to the south, contained in 1883 no old inscriptions.

In Memory of
MARY, wife of
EZEKIEL HAVENS;
who died June 30th,
1792, in the 30th year
of her age.

Elizabeth y𝑒 Daughter of George & Jemima Daval died Dec. 13th 1759 Aged 9 months.

FRANCES Daughter of James & Elizabeth Havens; died Augt 10th 1763 in the 2d year of her Age.

SARAH Daughter of James and Elizabeth Havens; died Augt 21st 1790 In the 5th year of her Age.

Time each moment plays
His little weapon in the narrow
Sphere
of sweet domeſtick Comfort
and cuts down
the faireſt Bloom of ſublunary
Bliſs.

SIDNEY
Son of
James & Elizabeth
Havens
was drowned Octr 6th 1789
In the 13th year of his Age
*(together with Mr. Samuel Stratten
to whom he was Apprentice)
They were lovely in their Lives
And in their Death
were not Devided.*

In Memory of
M William Havens
who departed this Life
May ye 4th 1763
In the 44th Year
of his Age

In Memory of
Sarah Wife of
William Havens
who died Octr 8th
1769
Aged 50 Years

In Memory of
Defire wife of
William Havens
& Daughter of William
& Sarah Havens who
died Novr 5th 1771
in the 22^d year of her age
*the Rifing Morning can't
Affure
that we fhall end the day
for death ftands ready
at the door
to fieze our lives away.*

Sacred to the Memory
of *Mifs Elmira Havens,*
Daughter of Obadiah
and Phebe Havens,
who departed this life
Feb. 27, 1779 in the 24
year of her age.
*With calm ferenity fhe clos'd
her eyes
On fublunary things.
Her foul took flight to worlds
beyond the fkies
On bright cherubic wings*

Here lyes ye Body of
Phebe Havens Dau^{tr}
of Mr William & M^{rs}
Sarah Havens, Who
Died Octo^{br} ye 28th
1752 in ye 4th Year
of her Age

IN MEMORY of
Jemima the Wife of
Mr George Daval
who died July ye 8th
A.D. 1761 in ye 66th
Year of her Age.

In Memory of
Mrs Anna Fofdick
Wife of
Doct^r Thos Fofdick
of New London
and Daughter of
Jonathan Havens Efq^r
of this Ifland,
who Died Sept 24th 1782
Aged 53 Years.

Here lyes ye Body of
Mary Ann Fofdick Daug^{tr}
of Mr Thomas & Mrs Anna
Fofdick, Who Died Jan^{ry} 11th 1753
Aged 10 Months & 12 Days
Save fruitlefs tears & weep no more
this Babe's not loft but gone before
Death's a Haven towards which
all winds drive
And where at laft each
Mortal muft arrive.

In Memory of
Obadiah Havens
who died Augt 22^d
1786
in the 40th year
of his Age
Blefsed are the Dead
that Die in the Lord

In
Memory of
WILLIAM Son of
JOSEPH & PHEBE
HAVENS who died
April 25th 1791
aged 14 years
and 10 mo.

In Memory of
OBADIAH HAVENS
who died
Aug. 22, 1787
Æ. 40.

CALEB HAVENS SALLY B. HAVENS
Son of Daughter of
AUGUSTUS & AUGUSTUS &
ESTHER HAVENS ESTHER HAVENS
died May 28th 1798 died Nov. 14th 1801
aged 1 month. aged 1 year 5 mo.
and 10 days.
Sleep lovely babes till Jefus comes
To raife his armyes from the tombs.

HERE LIES BURIED
THE BODY OF
Mrs FRANCES BAKER WIFE
TO Mr EPHRAIM BAKER
WHO DIED APRIL 24th
1758
AGED 21 YEARS

In Memory of
Mr Jonathan Havens
who died Novr 1st
AD. 1774
in the 66th year
of his Age

IN MEMORY of
Ellenor ye Wife of
Thomas Terry & formerly
ye Wife of George Havens
died Novem^r ye 7th 1747
in ye 93^d year
of Her age

IN MEMORY
of Hannah ye Wife
of Jonathan Havens
who died Augst ye 4th
1754 in ye 66th Year
of her Age

IN MEMORY
of Mr Jonathan Havens
who died Augst ye 5th
1748 in ye 68th year
of his age

In Memory of
Mrs MARGARET HAVENS
the Daughter of Mr JONATHAN
& Mrs CATHERINE HAVENS
who was Born Sunday Decemr
the 6th 1741 & departed
this Life on Thurfday the
23rd of Septembr 1762
Aged 20 Years 2 Months & 7 days

In Memory of Mrs
Catharine Havens
the wife of Mr
Jonathan Havens
who died May 4th
AD. 1779
in the 70th year
of her Age.

In Memory of
Mrs Sarah Havens
the Virtuous Wife of
Mr Nicoll Havens
who Departed this Life
the 4th Day of Auguft
ANNO DOMINI 1767 in the
37th Year of her Age

In Memory of
EASTER HAVENS
Daur of Mr NICOLL & Mrs
SARAH HAVENS who was
born Monday ye 4th of Septr
1759 & departed this life
on Wednesday the 4th of
Augst 1762   Aged 2
Years 11 Months

In Memory of
Henrietta Havens
Daughter of
Mr Nicoll and Mrs
Defire Havens
who died April 16th
AD   1784
in the 3d year
of her Age

[On white marble horizontal tablet on five supports.]

This Stone is erected
In Memory of
Jonathan Nicoll Havens, Efqr
a Reprefentative in the Congrefs
of the United States. He was efteemed
by a numerous acquaintance as a
man of fuperior talents and
erudition, a Philofopher, Statefman,
and Patriot, and died greatly
lamented Octr 25th AD 1799,
in the 42d year of his age.

[On brown-stone horizontal tablet supported by five columns.]

In Memory of
NICOLL HAVENS Esquire,
who died Septr 7th AD 1783
in the 51ft year of his age
In Memory of
SARAH, confort of
NICOLL HAVENS
who died Auguft 4th AD. 1767
in the 37th year of her age.

In Memory of
Watfon, Son of
Mr. Nicoll & Mrs.
Defire Havens
who died
March 11th 1785,
in the 6th Year
of his Age

In Memory of
Jofeph Havens
Son of M^r
Mr Jofeph and M^{rs}
Jemima Havens
who died Octr 13th
AD   1775,
in the 4th year
of his Age.

[On slate tablet inserted in brown-stone table-tomb.]

In Memory of
Mrs MARY HAVENS
the Virtuous Wife
of
Mr JOSEPH HAVENS
who departed this Life
the 20th day of Aug^{ft}
Anno Domni 1768
In the 76th year
of her Age.

In Memory of
Mr Jofeph Havens
who died May
AD   1775
in the 61st year
of his Age

In Memory of
Mrs Jemima Havens
the wife of M^r
Jofeph Havens
who died May 18
AD   1772
in the 28th year
of her Age

IN MEMORY OF
GEORGE HAVENS
SON OF M^r
GEORGE & M^{rs}
PATIANCE HAVENS
DIED DEC^R Y^e 2D 1754
AGED 6 MONTHS

IN MEMORY
of Patience ye Wife
of Mr George Havens
who died May ye 30th
1762 in the 38th Year
of her Age

IN MEMORY OF
JAMES CONKLING
son of M^r
THOMAS & M^{rs}
RACHEL CONKLING
DIED Octr 23D 1754
AGED 12 YEARS
5 MONTHS & 13 D^s

In Memory
of Ruth ye Wife of
William Havens
who died Feb 18
1759 in ye 39
Year of her Age

In Memory of
John Havens
who was drown
ed Oct^{br} 6th 1789
in the 34th year
of his Age

IN MEMORY of
Elizabeth the Wife
of Benjamin Woodruff
who died Novem^r 11
AD   1760 Aged
60 Years

In Memory of
DEBROAH PARKER
Dau^r of Mr ABRAHAM &
Mrs MARY PARKER who
died Octo^r the 16th 1761
Aged 2 Years
1 Month & 2 Days
Sweet Soul we leave the to thy reft
Injoye thy Jesus & thy God
tell wee from bands of Clay Releaft,
Spring out & Clime the Shineing Road

In Memory of
Sarah Hains
Wife of
Henry Hains
who died
Octr 28th 1796
aged 41 years
Alfo
her infant *Henry* aged
5 months was inter'd
by her fide

In Memory of
Frankling Davall
Son of William
Davall Junr & Mary
Davall he departed
this Life Dec^{br} 16th
A D 1780 Aged 2
years 4 months &
4 days
Memento Mori

[On two slate tablets, each 18x25 inches, leaded into the top of a brown-stone table-tomb on five supports.]

[Arms]

Here lies Interred the Remains of M^{rs}
Mary Sylvester the virtuous Confort
of Brindley Sylvester Efq. who departed
this Life March the 1st 1750/1 in the
49th year of her Age.

[Arms]

Here lies Interr'd the Remains
of *BRINLEY SYLVESTER ESQ^r*
who Departed this Life December the
24th 1752 In the 59th year of his Age.

[On a marble tablet set into the top of a brown-stone table-tomb.]

[Arms]

In Memory of
THOMAS DERING Esq.
who died Sep. 26, 1785
aged 65 years.
In Memory of
MARY DERING *relict of*
Tho. Dering and daughter
of Brinley & Mary Sylvester
who died Aug. 19, 1794
aged 70 years.

SYLVESTER MANOR.

In the northern part of the Island, and near the old Manor House of the Sylvesters, is the small family burial ground, containing in 1899 the table-tomb recently erected, and a few ancient brown-stone stones. This is probably the oldest burial place of the Island. The grave stones of the members of the Sylvester family were removed to the church yard in the middle of the Island many years ago.*

[On horizontal tablet of Table-tomb.]

TO

NATHANIEL SYLVESTER,

FIRST RESIDENT PROPRIETOR

OF

THE MANOR OF SHELTER ISLAND,

UNDER GRANT OF CHARLES II.

A.D. 1666;

[Arms]

AN ENGLISHMAN

INTREPID,

LOYAL TO DUTY,

FAITHFUL TO FRIENDSHIP,

THE SOUL OF INTEGRITY AND HONOR,

HOSPITABLE TO WORTH AND CULTURE,

SHELTERING EVER THE PERSECUTED FOR CONSCIENCE' SAKE;

THE DAUGHTERS

OF

MARY AND PHŒBE GARDINER HORSFORD,

DESCENDANTS OF

PATIENCE, DAUGTHER OF NATHANIEL SYLVESTER

AND

WIFE OF THE HUGUENOT BENJAMIN L'HOMMEDIEU

IN

REVERENCE AND AFFECTION

FOR

THE GOOD NAME OF THEIR ANCESTOR

IN 1884

SET UP THESE STONES

1610.   𝕱𝖔𝖗 𝖆 𝕸𝖊𝖒𝖔𝖗𝖎𝖆𝖑.   1680.

* The inscriptions from the family ground have been furnished through the courtesy of Miss Cornelia Horsford of Cambridge, and Miss Belle Preston, the librarian of the Shelter Island Public Library.

48

[Under the table.]
DESCENT FROM ANNE BRINLEY OF THE FEMALE SIDE.

[Arms]

THOMAS BRINLEY, King's Auditor, married ANNE WASE.
NATHANIEL SYLVESTER   married GRISSELL BRINLEY.
BENJAMIN L'HOMMEDIEU   married PATIENCE SYLVESTER.
BENJAMIN L'HOMMEDIEU, 2nd,   married MARTHA BOURNE.
EZRA L'HOMMEDIEU   married MARY CATHERINE HAVENS.
SAMUEL SMITH GARDINER   married MARY CATHERINE L'HOMMEDIEU.
EBEN NORTON HORSFORD   married MARY L'HOMMEDIEU GARDINER.

Succession of Proprietors.

THE MANHANSETT TRIBE.
THE KING.
THE EARL OF STIRLING.
JAMES FARRETT.
STEPHEN GOODYEAR.
NATHANIEL SYLVESTER.
GILES SYLVESTER.
BRINLEY SYLVESTER.
THOMAS DERING.
SYLVESTER DERING.
MARY CATHERINE L'HOMMEDIEU.
SAMUEL SMITH GARDINER.
EBEN NORTON HORSFORD.

[On the South Steps.]
Of the sufferings for conscience' sake of friends of
NATHANIEL SYLVESTER,
Most of whom sought shelter here, including
GEORGE FOX,
Founder of the Society of Quakers,
And of his followers,
MARY DYER,   MARMADUKE STEVENSON, and
WILLIAM ROBINSON,   WILLIAM LEDDRA,
Who were executed on Boston Common;

[On East Steps.]
LAWRENCE and CASSANDRA SOUTHWICK,
Despoiled, imprisoned, starved, whipped, banished,
Who fled here to die;

[On North Steps.]
DANIEL GOULD, bound to the Gun-carriage and lashed,
EDWARD WHARTON, "The much Scourged,"
CHRISTOPHER HOLDER, "The Mutilated,"
HUMPHREY NORTON, "The Branded,"
JOHN ROUS, "The Maimed,"
GILES SYLVESTER, "The Champion,"
RALPH GOLDSMITH, "The Shipmaster,"
SAMUEL SHATTUCK, of "The King's Missive,"
THESE STONES ARE A TESTIMONY.

[On West Steps.]
The Puritan in his pride, overcome by the faith of the Quaker, gave
LEXINGTON AND CONCORD AND BUNKER HILL
TO HISTORY.
The Blood and the Spirit of Victor and Vanquished alike are the Glory of
MASSACHUSETTS.

Samuel Hudfon
Son of Mr Samuel
and Mrs Grifevel
Hudfon Died Oct^br
7th 1738 Aged 11
years & 4 month^s

Nathaniel Hutfon
Son of Mr Samuel
& Mrs Grifeell
Hutfon died May
ye 26th 1733 in
ye 7th Year of
His Age

In memory of
Capt Daniel Brown
who died July 12
AD. 1786
in the 77 year
of his Age

Here Lieth ye Body of
Hannah ye wife of
Daniel Brown died
Septem^r ye 8 1731
In ye 23^d year of
her age

Here lyes ye Body of
Elizab^th Hudfon Dau^tr
of Mr Samuel & M^rs
Grifevel Hudfon Who
Died Sep^t 21st 1738 Aged
4 years 10 mon^ts & 11 Da^s

In memory of
Mrs Mary Brown
Relect of Capt.
Daniel Brown
who died
Sepr 5th 1796
in the 81 year
of her age

Here Lyes buried
ye Body of M^r
Jonathan Hutson
Who Dec^d April 5th
Anno Dom 1729
aged 71 years

Here lieth ye body of
Hannah ye daughter
of Daniel & Hannah
Brown died Febr^y
ye 26 1732
aged 6 M^o

Ebenezer ye Son
of Daniel & Mary
Brown died April
ye 25 1741 Aged
8 years 7 M^o
& 15 Days

[The epitaph of John Knowling, aged 73 years, is, for other particulars, illegible.]

EASTHAMPTON.

Of the two peninsulas forming the eastern end of Long Island, one half the length of the longer, terminating in what is known as Montauk Point, constitutes, with Gardiner's Island to the eastward, the township of East-hampton. From west to east this main portion of the town is twenty-three miles in length, its south side being an unbroken, straight stretch of beach, pounded unceasingly by the waves of the Atlantic Ocean. More than twelve miles of the easterly end consists of only a range of low sand hills, aver-aging hardly a mile in width, and containing no villages. Just west of this the land abruptly widens to six miles or more, the northern line broken by deep harbors from Gardiner's Bay. Within this wider portion of the town-ship lie the principal villages, Amagansett, Easthampton and Wainscott.

AMAGANSETT.

The home of the whale fishers, Amagansett, the eastern village of the township, is within sound of the ocean surf on the great south beach, and three miles east of the principal settlement, Easthampton. Its wide main street is crossed by another, leading to the ocean, and at their junction is the old burying ground, containing in 1887 the following inscriptions ante-dating 1800.

In
Memory of
Mr. Benjamin Eyres
who died
Decr 5th 1797
aged 84 years

In Memory of
Mrs. Elizabeth Deb-
ble Wife of Mr.
Thomas Debble
who died
Jan^{ry} 30th 1789
Aged 71 Years

In Memory of
Mary ye Wife of
Lewis Conkling
who died Novem^r
ye 15th 1752 in y^e
76th Year of
of [*sic*] her Age

In Memory of
Lewis Conkling
died Octob^r ye 2^d
A.D. 1746 in ye 74th
year of his Age

In Memory of
Samuel Mulford
who died
June 15th 1795
in the 82^d year
of his age

In Memory
of ZERUIAH
Wife of
SAMUEL MULFORD
departed this life
Novr 7th 1783
In the 68th Year
of her Age

In Memory of
Mary ye Wife
of Elias Mulford
who died July
29th 1762 in
ye 71^{ft} Year
of her Age

IN MEMORY of
Mr Elias Mulford
who died Nov^r
2^d 1760 in the
75th Year of
his Age

Henry Son
of Edward
and Deborah
Conkling
died Novr 23^d
1770 in y^e
4th Year of
his age

IN MEMORY of
Efther y^e Wife of
Mr Jonathan Baker
Junr & Daughter of
Mr John Parfons
who died Decr 6th
A.D. 1760 Aged
28 Years

Here
lies the Body of Efther
Ofborne Daughter of
Thomas Ofborne &
Efther Ofborne who
Died January y^e 16th
An. Dom. 17$\frac{38}{40}$ Aged
16 years & 6 months

Here lies
the Body of
David Baker who
Died Novemb^r y^e
23rd 1 7 2 9 In y^e
28th Year of His
Age

In Memory of
Lieu^t Jonathan
Baker died March
y^e 4th 1747/8 in y^e
69 Year of
his Age

Here lieth y^e Body
of Alice Baker Formeli
y^e Wife of Thomas
Baker Who Died
February ye 4 : 1708 : 9
In ye 88 year of Her
Age

HERE
LIES THE BODY OF
NATHANIEL BAKER
THE SON OF MISTER
THOMAS BAKER
WHO DYED FEBRUA
RY THE : 27 : AND IN
THE : 84 : TH YEAR OF
HIS AGE : 1738 / 9

Here Lieth ye Body
of Sarah ye Wife
of Nathaniel Baker
Who Died October
The 9 1727.   In ye 62
year of her Age.

Here lieth ye Body
of Catharin ye Wife
of Nathaniel Baker
Who Died May
ye 14 : 1722 : In y^e
66 year of Her
Age.

In Memory of
JULIA NABBY
Daughter of Davis
& Zeruiah Conklin;
who died
Jan^ry 28th 1800,
aged 5 years
Come read my date
And here you'll fee
No age nor fex from
death is free.

In Memory of
Samuel Mulford
died July ye 10th 1743
in ye 65th year
of his age

In Memory of
JULIA
Daughter of
Davis & Zeruiah
Conklin;
who died
Decr 16th 1792
aged 10 days

In
Memory of
ABIGAIL, Wife of
DANIEL CONKLIN;
who died
May 24, 1795
in the 70, year
of her age

In
Memory of
DANIEL CONKLIN
whe died
Octr 26. 1800
in the 83 year
of his age

Here lies
the Body of
Mrs Hannah widow
of Mr Benjamin
Conkling who died
June ye 29th 1752 in y^e
[broken off]

Here
Lies the
Body of M^r
Annanias Conkling
who died March ye 1
1740 in ye 68 year
of his Age

In Memory of
Mrs Efther Baker
Wife of M^r
Nathaniel Baker
who departed this
Life Septr 23d 1765
Aged 23 years

In Memory of
Mr Jeremiah
Conkling Who
Died July ye 21
A.D. 1746 Aged
28 years

In
Memory of
Henry Son of
Mr Daniel & M^rs
Mary Baker
Who Died May
ye 13th A.D. 1755

Here Liet The
Body of Achi
ld of ISAAC &
SARAH BARNS

In Memo
ry of Henry
Son of Mr Daniel
& Mrs Mary Bak
er Who Died Iu
ly ye 24th A.D.
1750

HERE
LIES THE
BODY OF
ISAIAH BARNS
WHO DIED JAN^ry
THE 27 · 1733 AGED
6 · YEARS · 4 · MONTHS
AND 3 DAS

IN MEMORY OF
ISAAC BARNS
Efq. who died
April y⁰ 22ᵈ 1772
in the 68ᵗʰ Year
of his Age
Death flew Commifsion'd
From on High
Nor warning Gave
Barns you muft die
Not Ufefulnefs
Itfelf can Save
Thy Life from the
Devouring Grave

Here
Lies the
Body of Mʳˢ
Sarah the wife of Mʳ
Isaac Barns junᵉʳ who
died October the 22
1736 Aged 38 years

EASTHAMPTON VILLAGE.

The village of Easthampton, the principal settlement in the township, is distant between three and four miles from the westerly line, and but a short distance from the south beach. The old burying ground is a long and narrow enclosure lying as it were in the middle of the main street. It is among the oldest, and most important, in an historical sense, in the county. In 1887 no other epitaphs of a date prior to 1800 were to be found there than these that follow.

Here lies depofited the
Remains of Mʳˢ
JERUSHA CONKLING
Confort of
ISAAC CONKLING Esqʳ
Confort firft of
DAVID GARDINER Esqʳ
and daughter of the Revᵈ
SAMUEL BUELL and
JERUSHA BUELL his Confort
fhe departed this Life
in hope of a better
Febʳʸ 24ᵗʰ 1782 in the
33ᵈ year of her Age

IN MEMORY
of the Revⁿᵈ Mʳ
Nathaniel Huntting
who died Septᵐʳ y⁰
21ᶠᵗ 1753 in y⁰ 78ᵗʰ
Year of his Age

Reader behold this Tomb
with Reverence and Regret!

Here lie the remains of
that EMINENT SERVANT
of CHRIST the REVEREND
SAMUEL BUELL D. D.
53 years Paftor of the Church
in this place. He was a faithful
and fuccefsful Minifter of the Gofpel
a kind relation, a true friend, a good
patriot, an honeft man and an
exemplary Chriftian
Was born Septr 1^ft 1716 died in peace
July 19th 1798 aged 82 years

They that turn many to righteoufnefs
fhall fhine as the brightnefs of the firma-
ment and the stars forever and ever
Remember them who have spoken unto
you the word of God whofe faith
follow confidering the end of their
converfation

IN MEMORY
of Jerufha ye Wife of
the Revd Samuel
Buell, who died
June 16th A.D. 1759
in ye 37th Year
of her Age

HERE LYES Y^e
BODY OF
PHEBE CURING
AGED 23 YEARS
DEC^D MAY Y^e 21
1 7 1 4

Here Lyes Buried
ye Body of M^r
SAMUEL CONKLING
Who Dec^d April
ye 30th 1726 in y^e
25th Year of his Age

Here Lyes Buried
the Body of Capt
SAMUEL MULFORD
Who Dec^d Auguft
ye 21^ft 1725 Aged
about 80 years

MARY DAU^R OF
ELIAS & MARY
MULFORD AGED
4 MONTHS & 18
DAYS DIED
MARCH Y^e 29th
1 7 1 8

Here Lyes ye Body of
Mrs ESTHER MULFORD
Wife of Capt SAMUEL
MULFORD Who Dec^d
Novem^br ye 24^rh 1717 in
ye 64th Year of Her Age

HERE LYES THE
BODY OF M^r
JEREMIAH CONKLING
AGED 73 YEARS
WHO DEPARTED THIS
LIFE AUGUST Y^e 9th
1 7 3 4

HERE LYES BURIED THE
BODY OF Mrs JANE
CONKLING WIFE OF M^r
JEREMIAH CONKLING
AGED 76 YEARS &
6 M^o WHO DIED
APRIL 21st 1741

Here lies y^e
Body of M^rs
Mercy ye wife
of Mr John Miller
Who Died July
ye 30th 1744 in y^e
35th Year of
her Age

In Memory of
Peter Buell Son
of the Rev^d
Samuel Buell &
Jerufha his Wife
who died June
2^d 1761 in ye 8th
Year of his Age

MULFORD.
JOHN, (JUDGE)
EARLIEST SETTLER OF THIS TOWN IN 1649
DIED ABOUT 1686 Æ 80 FATHER OF
CAPT. SAMUEL,
FOR MANY YEARS MEMBER OF THE
PROVINCIAL ASSEMBLY OF NEW YORK
DIED AUG. 21 1725 Æ. 80
WAS BURIED NEAR THIS STONE.
FATHER OF CAPT. MATTHEW,
DIED AP'L 28, 1774 Æ. 85,
FATHER OF COL. DAVID,
OF 2ND SUFFOLK CO. REG'T,
DIED DEC. 18, 1778, Æ. 56.
FATHER OF SERGEANT MATTHEW
OF 1ST SUFFOLK CO. REG'T,
DIED M'CH 24, 1845 Æ. 85,
FATHER OF CHARLES L.
OF RENSSELAER VILLE, N.Y.
DIED MAY 28, 1857 Æ. 71
FATHER OF ROBERT L. MULFORD
OF NEW YORK CITY WHO ERECTS THIS
STONE IN 1880.

HERE : LYETH
THE : BODY : OF : M^r
JEREMIAH : CONK=
LING : WHO : DYED
MARCH : THE : 14 : TH
ANNO : 1711=12 : IN
THE : 80 : TH : YEARE
OF : HIS : AGE*

HERE LYETH THE
BODY OF Mrs MARY
CONKLING WIFE OF
Mr JEREMIAH CONK
LING WHO DIED
JUNE Y^e 15th 1727
AGED [illeg.] YEARS

In Memory
of Hannah y^e
Daughter of
y^e Revd Samuel
Buell & Jerufha
his Wife who
died Apr^l 11th
1759 Aged
3 Months

In Memory
of Efther y^e
Daughter of y^e
Revd Samuel
Buell & Jerufha
his Wife who
died Novr 13th
1757 Aged
1 Year & 10 M^o

JERUSHA BUELL
DAU^R OF Y^e REV^D
Mr SAMUEL & M^{rs}
JERUSHA BUELL
AGED 1 YEAR & 4
M^o DIED JAN^{ry} 20th
1 7 4 8 / 9

In Memory of
Efther Daught'r
of ye Revd Samu-
el Buell & Jeru-
fha his Wife
who died June
ye 19th 1754
aged 2 Years

Here lyes Buried
the Body of
JONATHAN HUNTING
M.A. Who Departed this
Life Sep^t 3^d *Anno Dom*^{ni} 1750
in ye 36th Year of His Age

* [Age may be 80, 60, or possibly 50.]

56

Mary Hunting,
Daugh. of Doct^r
Edward and Mr^s
Marcy Hunting
Died April 11th
1745 Aged 1 Year
& 3 Months

Here lyes Buried
ye Body of Doct^r
EDWARD HUNTING
M.A. Who departed
this Life *April* ye 10th
*Anno Dom*ⁿⁱ 1745 in y^e
42nd Year of His Age

Edward Son of
Dr Edward and
Mercy Hunting
Dec^d Augst 9th
1738 Aged 4
Years & 10 Months

MARY DAU^R OF
NATHANIEL &
MARY HUNTING
AGED 4 M^o DIED
SEPT^r 19th 1706.

In Memory of
Samuel ye Son
of Eliphelet &
Phebe Stratten
who died Octo^r
12th 1753 in y^e
25th Year
of his Age

In Memory of
Phebe ye Daught'r
of Eliphelet &
Phebe Stratten
who died July
12th 1762 in y^e
30th Year of
her Age

In Memory of
Mary ye Daught'r
of Eliphelet &
Phebe Stratten
who died June
8th 1761 in ye 32^d
Year of Her Age

In Memory of
Deacon
Joſeph Oſborn
who died
Novr 21^{ſt} 1786
in the 82^d year
of his age

IN MEMORY of
Mr David Stratton
who died Jany 6th A.D.
1770 Aged 48 Years

In Memory of
Hannah Wife of
Deacon
Joſeph Oſborn
who died
Novr 5th 1775
in the 67th year
of her age

In Memory of
ABRAHAM Son of
Decon
JOSEPH OSBORNE
by HANNAH his
Wife he died Sept^r
the 15th 1772 in
the 30th Year of
his Age

In Memory of
Mrs. Mary Osborn
Wife of M^r Joſeph
Oſborn who died
Auguſt 9th 1783
aged 43 years
My fleſh ſhall ſlumber
in the ground,
Till the last trumpet's
joyful found
Then burſt the chains
with ſweet ſurpriſe
And in my Saviour's
image riſe.

In Memory of
Mr. Jofeph Ofborn
who died
April 2ᵈ 1798
in the 60ᵗʰ year
of his age

In Memory of
Mrs. Hannah
Hedges Relict of
Mʳ Jonathan Hed-
-ges, who died
Janʳʸ 12ᵗʰ 1792
in the 83ᵈ year
of her age

In Memory of
Mr. Lewis Ofborn
who died
Septʳ 14ᵗʰ 1783
aged 36 years

Robert L. Hedges
Son of Mr. Reuben
& Mrs. Hannah
Hedges : died
Febʸ 7ᵗʰ 1793
aged 5 months

In Memory of
Mr. Jeremiah Miller,
who departed
this life
July 11ᵗʰ 1794
in the 67ᵗʰ year
of his age
Behold and fee as you pafs by
As you are now fo once was I
As I am now you foon will be
Prepare for Death to follow me

Here lies the
Remains of
Peggy Negro
Servᵗ to *Capᵗ*
Abraham Gardiner
aged 22 years

In Memory of
Eleazer Miller
Efquire
who died March
15ᵗʰ 1788
in the 92ᵈ year
of his Age

Here lies Buried
the Body of
Matthias Burnet
Esqʳ who Died October
the 4ᵗʰ 174·5
in yᵉ 72ᵈ Year of his Age

HERE LYES BURIED
THE BODY OF Mʳ
ABRAHAM MEDE MA
WHO DIED NOVʳ 1ˢᵗ
1742 IN THE 21ˢᵗ
YEAR OF HIS AGE

HERE LIES BURIED
THE BODY OF Mʳˢ
MARY MILLER WIFE OF
ELEAZER MILLER ESQʳ
WHO DIED APRIL 14ᵗʰ
1743 IN THE 42ᴰ
YEAR OF HER AGE

IN MEMORY
of Elizabeth the
Wife of Matthias
Burnit Efqʳ who
died April 27ᵗʰ 1761
in the 86ᵗʰ Year
of her Age

IN MEMORY of
JOSIAH MILLER who
died Octoʳ 4ᵗʰ A.D. 1770
Aged 81 Years

HERE LIES BURIED
THE BODY OF Mʳˢ
TEMPERANCE HEDGES
WIFE OF Mʳ
WILLIAM HEDGES
DIED OCTᴿ 28ᵗʰ
1 7 5 3
AGED 36 YEARS

HERE LIES Yᵉ BODY OF
DAVID HEDGES
SON OF Mʳ
WILLIAM & Mʳˢ
TEMPERANCE HEDGES
DIED JUNE 23ᴰ
1 7 5 3
AGED 23 MONTHS
AND 23 DAYS

HERE LIES Yᶜ BODY OF PHEBE HEDGES DAUᴿ OF Mʳ WILLIAM &
Mʳˢ TEMPERANCE HEDGES DIED DECᴿ 13ᵗʰ 1753 AGED 1 MONTH AND
23 DAYS

In Memory of
Mʳ Jofiah Miller
who died
Auguſt 12ᵗʰ 1773
in the 49ᵗʰ year
of his age

IN MEMORY OF
SAMUEL MILLER
SON OF Mʳ
JEREMIAH & Mʳˢ
RUTH MILLER
DIED AUGˢᵗ 31ˢᵗ 1754
AGED 4 YEARS
& 22 Dˢ

Mary Daught'r
of Mʳ Eliſha &
Jeruſha Conk
ling died Decᵐʳ
yᵉ 16ᵗʰ 1756
aged 2 Years

IN MEMORY
of Jeruſha yᵉ Wife
of Mʳ Eliſha Coukling
Junʳ who died May
yᵉ 30ᵗʰ A.D. 1757
in yᵉ 33ᵈ Year
of her age

In Memory of
Phebe yᵉ Wife of
Mʳ Jofiah Miller
who died Septʳ 12ᵗʰ
1758 in yᵉ 62ᵈ Year
of her age

In Memory of
Elizabeth yᵉ Wife
of Benjamin Ayers
who died April 1ᶠᵗ
1757 in yᵉ 30ᵗʰ Year
of her Age

IN MEMORY of
JOSIAH HEDGES
who died July 26ᵗʰ
A.D. 1767 in the
41ˢᵗ Year of
his Age

In Memory of
Mʳ JOHN HEDGES
who died March
12ᵗʰ 1786
in the 86ᵗʰ year
of his Age

[A footstone to grave next that of John Hedges is marked D.H. 1769.]

IN MEMORY of
ELIZABETH the
wife of JOHN
HEDGES who
Died April the 18ᵗʰ
A.D. 1772 in the
69ᵗʰ Year of
Her Age

In Memory of
JOHN Son of
Mʳ Jofiah & Mʳˢ
Mary Hedges;
who died
Auguſt 28th.
1 7 7 8
aged 12 years

Jofiah Son of
Daniel & Jeruſha
Hedges who
died May yᵉ 22ᵈ
1769 Aged 6
weeks & 6 Days

Samuel Son of
Mʳ Jonathan &
Zervia Hedges
who died Janʳʸ
14ᵗʰ 1 7 7 1
Aged 4 Years
& 1 Mᵒ

In Memory of David Hedges Son of Mr. Jonathan & Mrs. Zerviah Hedges who
died Janʳʸ 19ᵗʰ 1777 in the 9ᵗʰ year of his Age.

In Memory of Temperance Hedges Daughter of Mr. Jonathan & Mrs. Zerviah
Hedges who died July 22d 1777 in the 17th year of her age.

IN MEMORY
of Deacon JOHN
HUNTING who
died March 14th 1768
in the 61st Year of
his Age
This was his farewell dying Word
Tis blefsed dying in the Lord;
How great such Blefseduefs will be,
He left this World and went to see.

In Memory of
CLEMENCE HUNTTING
the Wife of Deacon
John Huntting
who died July 19, A.D.
1776 in the 71ft Year
of her Age

In Memory of
Mrs. Zerviah Hed-
-ges Relict of Mr.
Jonathan Hedges
who died
March 8th 1792
in the 56th year
of her age

IN MEMORY of
Elizabeth ye Wife
of Burnet Miller
Efqr who died May
ye 16th 1765 in the
37th Year of her Age

In Memory of
Mr *AARON ISAACS*
who died Septr 11th
1797, in the 75th year
of his age

In Memory of CLARRY Daughter of *Mr.* Aaron & *Mrs. Efther Isaacs* who died Decr 5th 1789 aged 3 years 2 mo. & 5 days.

In Memory of CLARISSA only Daughter of *Mr. Aaron & Mrs Efther Isaacs* who died Octr 27th 1798 aged 7 years 8 months and 9 days.

Sarah Daughter of Mr Henry & Mrs Annie Chatfield died April 15th 1783 in the 8th Year of her Age.

MAJ. DAVID MULFORD
died Jan. 8, 1799
Æ. 42.

Jonathan
Son of Capt
David Mulford
& Phebe his
Wife died Apr
27th 1768
Aged 6 Mo
& 10 Days

In Memory of Mrs.
ELISABETH MULFORD
daughter of
Col. DAVID & Mrs
PHEBE MULFORD
who died July 21st
A D. 1785,
in the 23d year
of her Age

In Memory of Col.
DAVID MULFORD
who died Decr 18th
A D: 1778:
in the 57th year
of his Age

Juliana Mulford
Daughter of Mr
Matthew & Mrs.
Mary Mulford
died Janry 24th
1793
aged 11 years.

Abraham Dayton
Son of Elifha &
Elifabeth Conkling
who died March
27th A.D. 1770
Aged 10 Months

Silvanus Son of
Annanias &
Lucretia Miller
who died Novr
6th 1771 Aged
5 Years & 6 Days

In Memory of
Samuel Son of
Jeremiah Miller
& Mary his Wife
born & died July
4 A. D. 1774
J : S,

In Memory of
MARY MILLER
Wife of
JEREMIAH MILLER jun^r
who died July 8 A.D.
1785 in the 33^d Year
of her Age.

In Memory of
Lieut. John Dayton
who departed this
life Jan^{ry} 27th 1789,
in the 35th year
of his age.
*Oh ! what a free a mercy
this
That Death a portal into
bliſs
Before the body is
ondreſt
The Soul is ſlipt into its
reſt.*

In Memory of
THOMAS M.
WICKHAM ESQ^r
who died Auguſt 14th
AD. 1790
In the 60th Year
of his Age.

In Memory of
Edward Son of
Thomas Wickham Esqr
& Marcy his Wife
who died Octob^r 18
1775 aged 5 years &
22 days.

In Memory of
Mrs. Mary Oſborn
Wife of Capt
Jeremiah Oſborn
who died
Jan^r 31^{ſt} 1797
aged 41 Years 3
months & 29 days

In Memory of
William R.
Hedges Son of
Mr. Daniel and
Mrs. Jeruſha
Hedges who died
June 21^{ſt} 1794
aged 1 year
and 8 months.

HERE LIES BVRED Y^e
BODY OF Mrs ELIZEBETH
GARDINER WIFE OF CAP^{TN}
SAM^L GARDINER WHO
DIED OCTOBER Y^e 1
1725 IN Y^e 22 YEAR
OF HER AGE
[Horizontal brown-stone tablet on brick base.]

IN MEMORY of
COL^{NL} ABRAHAM GARDINERS
Who
VAULT
departed this life Aug^{ſt} 21^{ſt} 1782
In the 62^d year of his Age
*Thus all we ſee like all we have
Of Good beneath the Skies ;
Shall reſt like that within this Grave
Till GOD ſhall ſay ariſe.*
[Horizontal brown-stone tablet on brick base. A prior inscription read
" COL^{NL} ABRAHAM GARDINER'S VAULT."]

HERE LYETH THE BODY OF
CAPᵀ SAMᴸ GARNAR WHO
DECEASED MAY 24 1729
AGED 31 YEARS.
[Horizontal tablet on brick base.]

HERE LYETH THE
BODY OF Mʳˢ MARY
GARDINER THE WIFE
OF Mʳ IOHN GARDINER
OF THE ISLE OF WIGHT
DIED Yᵉ 4 DAY OF IVLY
1707 AND IN THE
THIRTYEIGHT YEAR OF
HER AGE

[Horizontal brown-stone tablet. Its brick base supports also the stone covering the vault of Col. Abraham Gardiner. Still another tablet on base, next beside this, is without inscription.]

HERE LYETH
the Body of Mʳˢ
Rachel Gardiner
Wife to his Excellʸ
David Gardiner Esqʳ
Lord of the Isle of
Wight who was
Married April 15
A: D 1713, and
departed this life
Dec. 16, A: D. 1744.

[Inscription on a piece of fine red slate, 18 x 22 inches, with conventional scroll border, set into the upper surface of a brown-stone table tomb on five columns.]

In Memory
of
Capᵗ Abraham Gardiner
who died
Octʳ 12ᵗʰ 1796
in the 34ᵗʰ year
of his age.
[Horizontal tablet on brick base.]

HERE LIES
DR. NATHANIEL GARDINER
During the Revolution
A surgeon in the American Army
Subsequently for several years
A *Representative* from this County
in the Legislature of the State;
and at a later period
a shipping merchant
in the City of New York.
He was born Jan: 11, 1759,
And died March 25, 1801.

In the adjoining graves
Lie the remains of
ELIZABETH, his wife,
Daughter of Thomas Dering, Esq.
who died March 18, 1801, Æ. 44;
And of
MARIA SYLVESTER,
their daughter,
who died Nov. 9, 1804, Æ. 20.

ROBERT SMITH, SON OF
Nathaniel & Eliza Gardiner
Born at East-Hampton
Sept. 10, 1786,
Died in New York Jan. 19, 1824, Æ. 37.
[Horizontal brown-stone slab on brick base.]

In
Memory of
Mrs. Mary Gardiner,
widow of
Col. Abraham Gardiner
and Daughter of
Nathaniel Smith Esq.
and of his wife
Phebe Howell;
she died May 19, 1807
in the 82 year
of her age.

In Memory of
MIfs PHEBE GARDNER
Daughter of Col.
ABRAHAM & Mrs
MARY GARDINER
who departed this life
Sepr 18 AD. 1775
in the 20th year of her age.
Time was, like thee I life Pofsefs
And time fhall be when thou
muft reft.

In Memory of
John Son of
Mr John & Mrs
Elifabeth Gard-
ner who decd
APril 22nd 1747
1 Year 10 months &
16 days old

IN MEMORY OF
Mrs ELIZABETH GARDINER
WIFE OF THE HONble
JOHN GARDINER LORD
OF THE ISLE OF WIGHT
DIED OCTr 21st 1754
AGED 40 YEARS
AND 2 MONTHS

Samuel ye Son
of Jeremiah &
Mary Gardiner
died Augft 12th.
1753   Aged 18
Mo & 2 Days

John ye Son
of John &
Elizabeth
Gardiner
died Octor 16th
1752 in ye 4th
Year of his Age.

IN MEMORY OF
MATTHEW MULFORD
Efqr who died April
28th A.D.   1774
in the 85th Year
of his Age.

IN MEMORY OF
Mrs ELIZABETH MULFORD
THE WIFE OF CAPT
MATTHEW MULFORD
DIED SEPt 11th 1754
IN THE 67th YEAR
OF HER AGE

IN MEMORY
of Efther the Wife of
Doctr John Darbe A: M.
who died Septemr 24th
A.D. 1757 Aged
38 Years & 2 Months

IN MEMORY of
SARAH Wife
of Mr SAMUEL
MULFORD
who died April
6th 1760 in ye
97th Year of
her Age

IN MEMORY of
ELIZABETH
Wife of Mr
LEWIS CONKLING
who died Octor
30th 1765 in ye
61ft Year of
her Age

Here Lyes Buried
the Body of Mr
AARON FITHIAN
Who Departed this life
May 1ft A.D. 1750 in ye
66th Year of His Age

Efther Daughter
of David &
Efther Fithian
died Jany 23d
1753   Aged
5 Years

HERE LYES Y^e
BODY OF MIRIAM
FITHIAN WIFE
OF ENOCH FITHIAN
WHO DEPARTED
THIS LIFE APRIEL
Y^e 1 1717
AGED 61 YEARS

IN MEMORY OF LION GARDNER.

An offic^er of ye Englifh Army and An Engine^er Maft^er of Work^es of Fortifications in Y^e Leagu^ers of ye Prince of Orang^e in ye Low Countri^es — In 1635 h^e cam^e to New England

In ye S^ervice of a Company of Lords & G^entl^em^en h^e bvild^ed & Command^ed ye Saybrook Fort^e.

Aft^er compl^eting this t^erm of s^ervic^e h^e r^emov^ed in 1639 to his If-land of which h^e was fol^e Owner & P.vlr^e. Born in 1599 h^e di^ed in this Town^e in 1663 Ven^erat^ed and honour^ed.

Und^er many trying Circumftanc^es in P^eac^e and War h^e was Brav^e Discre^et & Trve.

[Cut on the four sides—north, west, south and east—of a pretentious modern canopy tomb, with recumbent figure of a man in armor.]

IN MEMORY of
Nathan Dayton
who died Octo^r
3^d A.D. 1763 in
ye 61^{ft} Year of
His age

IN MEMORY
of Amey Wife of
Nathan Dayton
who died Sept^r
25th A.D. 1749
in the 51^{ft} Year
of Her Age

HERE
LYES THE
BODY OF DEBORAH
DAYTON WIFE TO
DANIEL DAYTON
WHO DECEASED NO
VEMBER THE 6 1717
AGED 24 YEARS

Here Lyes Buried
ye Body of Samuel
Dayton Son of Mr Samuel
& Mrs Dorothy Dayton
Who Dec^d April y^e
23^d 1726 in ye 20th
Year of Her Age.

In Memory of M^r
Samuel Gardiner
Son of M^r
Samuel Gardiner Merc^t
of New London he was
born Octr 10th 1758 &
died Feb^{ry} 1st 1789
Aged 30 years.
In early life Death laid me down
Here to await the trumpet's found
When God commands I will arife
to meet my Saviour in ye fkies
& while you read the ftate of me
think on the Glafs that runs for
thee.

Here lyes Buried
yᵉ Body of Mʳ
JOSEPH KING
Who Departed this
Life Novʳ 6ᵗʰ 1732 iu yᵉ
26ᵗʰ Year of His Age

Here Lyes Buried yᵉ
Body of Mʳˢ DOROTHY
DAYTON Widow of
Mʳ SAMUEL DAYTON
Who Departed this
Life March 22ᵈ 1750 in yᵉ
86ᵗʰ Year of Her Age.

HERE
LYES THE BODY
OF MEHETEBEL
BROWN WHO DE-
CEASED AVGVST
THE 26 1712
AGE 17 YEARS

HERE LYES Yᵉ BODY OF
Mʳˢ ELIZABETH OSBORN
WIFE OF Mʳ WILLIAM
OSBORN WHO DEPARTED
THIS LIFE OCTOBER
Yᵉ 14ᵗʰ 1744 IN Yᵉ 53ᴅ
YEAR OF HER AGE

HERE LYES Yᵉ BODY
OF Mʳˢ SUSANNA
DAYTON WIFE OF Mʳ
BERIAH DAYTON JUNʳ
WHO DEPARTED THIS
LIFE JULY Yᵉ 22ᴅ
1743 IN Yᵉ 31ˢᵀ
YEAR OF HER AGE

In Memory of Mʳ
Beriah Dayton
Who Died April
yᵉ 30 A.D. 1746
Aged 74 years

In Memory of
Mʳˢ Jain Relict to
Mʳ Beriah Dayton
Who Died Febʳʸ
yᵉ 21 A.D. 1754
Aged 79 years

In Memory of
Joanah yᵉ Wife of
Mʳ John Dayton
who died Septemʳ
22 1752 in yᵉ 53ᵈ
Year of her Age

IOSEPH : SON
OF : Mʳ NATHᴸ &
MARY HUNTING
DIED AUG: ¹⁴ 1711
AGED [illegible]

HERE LYES BURIED
Yᵉ BODY OF Mʳˢ MARY
HUNTTING WIFE OF Yᵉ REVᴰ
Mʳ NATHANIEL HUNTTING
OF EASTHAMPTON OCTᴿ 7ᵗʰ
1733 AGED 54
YEARS & About 5 Mᵒ

HERE LYES Yᵉ BODY OF ELIZABETH HUNTTING Yᵉ DAUʳ OF M
NATHANIEL & Mʳˢ MARY HUNTTING WHO DIED JULY Yᵉ 7ᵗʰ 1719 AGED
8 MONTHS
MARY HUNTTING Yᵉ DAUʳ OF Mʳ NATHˡ HUNTTING JUNʳ & MARY
HIS WIFE AGED 3 YEARS 3 Mᵒ & 20 Dˢ DYED AUGˢᵗ 30ᵗʰ 1738
JOSEPH HUNTTING Yᵉ SON OF Mʳ NATHᴸ HUNTTING JUNᴿ & MARY
HIS WIFE AGED 6 YEARS 9 Mᵒ & 20 Dˢ DYED SEPᵀ 30ᵗʰ 1738.

HERE LYETH YE
BODY OF MR
JOSEPH OSBORN
DIED OCTOBER YE 2ᴺᴰ
1743 IN Yᵉ 83ᴿᴰ
YEAR OF HIS AGE
[Inscription has been recut; possibly
the stone is modern.]

In Memory
of Mʳˢ Mary
Ofborn Relict of
Mʳ Jofeph Ofborn
who died Auguft
yᵉ 2ⁿᵈ A.D. 1752 in yᵉ
81ˢᵗ Year of her Age

65

HERE
LYETH THE
BODY OF IOHN
DAYTON SON
OF ROBERT AND
HANNAH DAYTON
WHO DIED IVNE
THE 13th 1714
AGED 12 YEARS

HERE
LYETH
THE BODY OF
HANNAH DAYTON
DAVGHTER OF
ROBERT AND
HANNAH DAYTON
WHO DIED APRIL
THE 9th 1712
AGED 16 YEARS

MR
THOMAS
IAMES DYED
THE 16 DAY OF
IVNE IN THE
YEARE 1696 HE
WAS MINISTAR
OF THE GOSPELL
AND PASTURE
OF THE CHVRCH
OF CHRIST

[The position of this grave is singular—the head towards the east,—tradition says, by the direction of its occupant. The other graves are with the heads towards the west.]

IN MEMORY of
Eliphelet Stratten
who died Septr
21st A.D. 1753
Aged 60 Years

HERE LIES
THE BODY OF
THOMAS OSBOND
WHO DIED SEPTEMBER
23 : 1712 AGED
89 YEARS

In Memory of
Cornelius ye Son
of Eliphelet &
Phebe Stratten
who died Septr
15th 1742 in ye
26th Year of
his Age

HERE
LYES
THE BODY OF
DANIELL OSBOND
WHO DEPARTED
IANUARY Ye 6
1712 AGED 48
YEARS

IN MEMORY
of John Mulford
Junr died March
ye 5th 1761 in ye
29th Year of
his Age

TALMAGE GOOLDE
Ye SON OF SEVERUS
& PHEBE GOOLDE
AGED 2 YEARS 7
Mo & 5 Ds DECd
JULY Ye 5th 1726

Here Lyes ye
Body of
Mr NATHAN
MULFORD
Who Decd Octobr
ye 13th 1723 Aged
35 Years &
about 2 Months

Here lyes THE
body of Phebe
Mulford aged
8 years &
11 Months dec⁴
March THE 21ˢᵗ
1723

In Memory of
Annah yᵉ Wife of
John Mulford Efqᵗ
who died March 13ᵗʰ
1759 in yᵉ 50ᵗʰ Year
of his Age

HERE
LIES THE
BODY OF THOMAS
SON OF ONESSIMUS
TALᴸMAGE WHO DEPAR
TED THIS LIFE NOVEM
BER THE 13ᵗʰ 1722 AGED
18 YEARS 5 MONTHS
AND 27 DAYS

HERE
LYETH Yᵉ
BODY OF CATAIN
ONESSIMUS TALᴸ
MAGE WHO DEPARTED
THIS LIFE FEBREVRY
Yᵉ 1ˢᵗ 1722 AGED 61
YEARS 1 MONTH
AND SIX DAYS

Temperance yᵉ
Daughter of Mʳ
Sweeten Grant
& Margaret his
Wife died May
yᵉ 28ᵗʰ 1757
Aged 14 Mᵒ
& 2 Days

In Memory
of Phebe Daughᵗ
of Mʳ Jofeph &
Mʳˢ Hannah
Thorne who died
Decemʳ 29ᵗʰ 1752 in
yᵉ 2ᵈ year of her Age

In
Memory of
Jonathan Son to
Mʳ Jonathan & Mʳˢ
Elifabeth Ofborn
Died Auguft 31
A.D. 1757 Aged 4
years 5 months

In
Memory of
Mary Daughter
of Mʳ Jonathan
& Mʳˢ Elifabeth
Ofborn Died
Ianua 23 A.D. 1759
Aged 4 Months
& 9 Days

Joseph Osborn
son of Mʳ
Joseph & Mʳˢ
Hannah Osborn
aged 1 months died
Septᵗ 1734

IN MEMORY of
HANNAH Wife of
JESSE DAYTON
she died March yᵉ
19ᵗʰ A.D. 1771 in the
36ᵗʰ Year of her Age

John Son of
John & Tempe-
rence Miller
died
Janrʸ 24ᵗʰ
1765 Aged
about 3 Mᵒ

IN MEMORY
of Temperance
the Wife of John
Miller Junʳ who
died Nov 1ˢᵗ 1764
in the 24ᵗʰ Year
of her Age

In
Memory of
An Infant Son
of Mʳ Jonathan
& Mʳˢ Elifabe
th Ofborn Died
Nov'r 29 A.D.
1752 Aged 7
Days

IN MEMORY
of Deacon Daniel
Ofburn who died
May yᵉ 17ᵗʰ A.D. 1757
in yᵉ 65ᵗʰ Year
of his Age
Blefsed are the dead
which die in the Lord

IN MEMORY of
JANE Wife of
THOMAS OSBORN
she died March
the 8th A.D. 1758 in
the 38th Year of her
Age

In Memory of
Thomas Ofborn
who died Decem^r
27th 1753 in y^e
41ft Year of
his Age

IN MEMORY of
David Baker Efq^r
who died April 7th
A.D. 1774 Aged
43 Years 8 M^o and
17 Days

In Memory of
Deborah Daught'r
of Thomas &
Jane Ofborn
who died Nov^r
ye 29th 1753 in
ye 12th Year of
her Age.

In Memory of
M^r
DAVID BAKER
who departed this
Life April 17 A.D.
1784 in the 21ft Year
of his Age

In Memory of NATHAN Son of David Baker Efq^r & Mehitabel, his Wife, who died March 6th 1774 Aged 1 Year 6 M^o & 23 Days.

In Memory of NATHANIEL Son of David Baker Efq. & Mehitabel his Wife who died Septr 9th 1771 aged 2 M^o & 16 Days.

In Memory of ELIZABETH Daughter of David Baker Efq^r & Mehetable his Wife who died Aug^{ft} 29th 1770 Aged 20 Days.

In Memory of PHEBE Daughter of David Baker Efq^r & Mehitabel his Wife who died Feby 23^d 1770 Aged 1 Year 9 M^o & 10 Days.

In Memory of Phebe Daughter of David & Mehitable Baker who died Feb^{ry} 16th A: D. 1767 Aged 2 M^o & 27 Days.

Nathan Son of Samuel & Joanna Baker died June 20th 1763 Aged 4 M^o & 20 Days.

In Memory of MARY BAKER Daughter of DAVID BAKER Efq^r & MEHETABLE his wife who died March 15, 1775 in the 5th Year of her Age.

IN MEMORY of
Joanna the Wife
of Samuel Baker
who died Octo^r 5th
A.D. 1763 Aged
26 Years &
6 Months

IN MEMORY of
Nathaniel Youngeft
Son of Nathaniel
Baker Efq^r who died
Janr^y the 23^d A.D.
1771 in the 27th Year
of his Age

Nathaniel Baker Son
of Nathaniel Baker
Efq^r & Mrs Sarah
his Wife Died Sep^t
24th 1743 Aged 17
Months & 24 Days

Here lyes ye Body
of Mr Thomas
Baker Who Departed
this Life Septem^r
ye 8th 1735 in y^e
82^d Year of his Age

In Memory of
Nathan ye Son of
Nathanael Baker
Efq^r & Sarah his
Wife who died
Jan^{ry} ye 11th 1759
in ye 22^d Year of
his Age

Nathan Baker Son
of Nathaniel Baker
Efq^r & Mrs Sarah
his Wife Who Died
by the Fall of a Tree
May 9th 1737 Aged 11
years 2 M^o & 27 D^s

IN MEMORY of
SARAH BAKER the
Wife of NATHANIEL
Baker Efq^r who died
Decem^r 12th A.D. 1768
Aged 63 Years and
16 Days

Here lies Interr'd
the Body of M^{rs}
Elizabeth Baker
Relict of M^r
Thomas Baker
who died July y^e
18th 1753 in ye 84th
year of her Age

IN MEMORY of
NATHANIEL BAKER
Efq^r who died Jan^{ry} 14th
A.D. 1772, Aged
72 Years 11 Months
And 27 Days

IN MEMORY
of Hannah & her
Babe ye Wife & Babe
of Mr Abraham
Talmage who died
May 30th A.D. 1763
in ye 21^{ft} Year
of her Age

In Memory of
Mary Daughter
of Daniel &
Rachel Dayton
who died Octo^r
6th 1757 Aged
2 Years 5 M^o
& 29 Days

IN MEMORY of
Mr Daniel Dayton
who died Septr ye 4th
A.D. 1762 in ye 68th
Year of his Age

In Memory of
Mifs Jane Ofborn
Daughter of M^r
Thos & Mrs Jane
Ofborn, who died
March 27th 1776
in the 30th Year
of her Age

In Memory of
Thomas Son of
Cornelius &
Hannah Ofborn
who died
April 3^d 1795

Juliana Daughter
of Mr Cornelius
& Mrs Hannah
Ofborn died
Decr 18th 1790
Aged 3 months
& 1 day

Thomas, Son of
Mr Thomas &
Mrs Phebe Ofborn
died in the year
1776 in the 7th
year of his Age

In Memory of
Mrs. Phebe Miller
Wife of *Mr.*
John Miller Junr
who died
Novr 17th 1798
in the 31^{ft} year
of her age

In Memory of
Mrs. Mary Ofborn
Wife of Mr. Jofeph
Ofborn who died
Novr 7th 1793
aged 60 years
*What finners value
I refign
LORD 'tis enough
that thou art mine.*

In Memory of
Mr.
Daniel Ofborn
who died
Decr 4th 1792
in the 73^d year
of his Age

In Memory of
Mr Thomas Ofborn
who departed this
Life in the year
of our Lord 1787
Aged 43 years

In
Memory of
Daniel Dayton Ju^r
who died
Decr 1, 1798
in the 42 year
of his age

In Memory of
Mrs. Rachel Dayton
Wife of *Deac*^u
Daniel Dayton
fhe died
Jan. 6th 1794
in the 68th year
of her age

In Memory of
Mrs. JOANNA
Wife of Mr.
ABRAM COAN
who died
Octo^r 29, 1757
In her 24th
Year

Elifabeth
daughter of
Jeremiah and
Marcy Ofborn
died Sepr 19
1747 Aged
3 years

In Memory of
Mrs Marcy Ofborn
Wife of M^r
Jeremiah Ofborn
who departed this
Life Octr 5th 1767
Aged 62 years

In Memory of
Mr Jeremiah Ofborn
who departed this
Life Auguft 24th
1 7 7 5
in the 69th year
of his Age

In Memory of
Hannah ye Wife of
Lieu^t Jonathan
Baker dece^ft & Sifter
of John Davis who
died June 9th 1757
in ye 77th Year of
her Age

IN MEMORY
of Mr JOHN DAVIS
who died Aug^ft ye 3^d
A.D. 1766 in the 91^ft
Year of his Age

In Memory
of Mr Jonathan
Stratton who Depart-
ed this Life Decemb^r
the 14th A.D. 1755
In the 48th Year of
his Age

In Memory of
Mr. Noah Barns
who died
Decr 27th AD. 1794
aged 91 years
and 2 months
[Grave stone of Mrs. Hannah, wife of Mr. Noah Barns is near by.]

In Memory of
Noah Barns jun^r
Son of Mr Noah
and Mrs Hannah
Barns who died
Octob^r ye 26 1753
In the 21st year
of his Age

IN MEMORY
of Efther ye Wife of
Mr Elifha Conkling
who died Octob^r
ye 26th A.D. 1756
in ye 58th Year
of her Age

IN MEMORY of
Mr Elifha Conkling
Who Died Febr^y 15th
A.D. 1772 Aged 81
Years & 11 Months

IN MEMORY
of Mr Benjamin
Conkling who
died June ye 6th
1764 Aged
29 Years

IN MEMORY of
MARY the Daughter
of STEPHEN and
MARY HEDGES
who Departed
this Life Feb^{ry} the
17th A.D. 1768 in
the 19th year of
her Age

Here
lies the Body
of Mrs Mary Conkling
the wife of M^r
Ananias Conkling
who died Decem^r
the 6 1750 in the 40th
Year of her Age

IN MEMORY
of Mr WILLIAM
HEDGES who
departed this
Life Novr the 4th
1768 in the 89th
year of his Age

IN MEMORY of
Abiah the Wife of
William Hedges
who died Octo. 27th
A.D: 1763 in ye 78th
Year of her Age

In Memory of
Mr Jacob Conkling
who died Novem^r
ye 6th 1753 in y^e
28th Year of
his Age

In Memory of
Mrs. Elizabeth
Miller Wife of
Mr. Huntting
Miller who died
Febr^y 1^{ft} 1792
in the 39th Year
of her Age

Sarah the
Daughter of
Mulford &
Ruth Conkling
died April y^e
15th 1757 Aged
1 Year 5 M^o
& 24 Days

HERE LYES THE
BODY OF M^r
NATHAN CONCKLING
SON OF Mr ELISHA
CONCKLING WHO
DIED OCTOBER Y^e 9th
1746 IN Y^e 23^D
YEAR OF HIS AGE

HERE LIES BURIED
THE BODY OF CAP^T
CORNELIUS CONKLING
WHO DIED OCT^R Y^e 30th
ANNO DOMINI 1748
IN THE 84th YEAR
OF HIS AGE

HERE : LYETH
THE : BODY : OF : M^{rs}
MARY : CONKLING
WIFE : OF : CAP^T : COR=
NELIVS : CONKLING
WHO : DYED : AVGVST
THE : 13 : TH : ANNO : 1712
IN : THE : 44 : TH : YEARE
OF : HER : AGE

HERE
LYETH THE
BODY OF MARY
DIBELL THE
WIFE OF GEORGE
DIBEL^L WHO DYED
THE 8 DAY OF
IANVARY AGED
23 YEARS 1705 : 6

JEREMIAH HEDGES
SON OF M^r
WILL^m & M^{rs}
TEMPERANCE HEDGES
AGED 6 MONTHS
& 10 D^s DIED
SEP^T 30th 1742

HERE
LYETH : THE
BODY : OF : ANTHONY
LVDLAM : WHO
DYED : MAY : THE 3rd
1716 : IN : THE : 17TH
YEAR : OF : HIS : AGE

HERE
LYES THE
BODY OF HANNAH
CONKLING WHO
DIED SEPTEMBER
Y^e 12 1720
AGED. 13 YEARS

IN MEMORY OF
CATHERIN DAU^r OF M^r
AARON & M^{rs}
MARY ISAACS
DIED JULY 10th 1751
AGED 6 MONTHS
& 5 D^s

In Memory
of Abigail Daugh^r
of Mr Daniel and
Mrs Abigail
Conkling died
Febr^y ye 19th 1753
in the 6th year
of her Age

IN MEMORY of
JOHN Son of
John & Elizabeth
Hedges who died
Septr 18th A.D. 1742
Aged 21 Years
And 10 Months

HERE LIES BURIED
THE BODY OF
Mr JOHN HEDGES
AGED 67 YEARS
DEC^D JANUARY 9th
1737

HERE : IS
THE : BODY : OF
MARY : HEDGES
WHO : WAS : DAVG
HTER : OF : JOHN
AND : RVTH : HEDGES
WHO : DYED : AVGS^T
THE : 10TH : ANNO : 1712
IN : THE : 13TH : YEAR
OF : HER : AGE

In Memory
of Abraham
Stratton 2 years
Old & Mehitable
Stratton 18 days Old
who died on ye 25th
and 26th of Sepr 1738
Son and Daughter of
Mr Jonathan and M^{rs}
Mehitable Stratton

In Memory of
Thomas Chatfield
Junr Efq^e died
Janr^y ye 1^{ft} 1742/3
In ye 31^{ft} year
of his age

IN MEMORY OF
THOMAS CHATFIELD Esqr
DIED JAN^R 13th
1754
IN THE 68th YEAR
OF HIS AGE

Here
lies the
Body of
Abraham Stratton
fon of Mr Jonathan
& Mrs Mehitable
Stratton he died
Augft ye 20th 1752 in
ye 9th year of his Age

IN MEMORY OF
Mrs HANNAH CHATFIELD
RELICT OF
THOMAS CHATFIELD ESQr
DIED AUGft 26th 1754
IN THE 68th YEAR
OF HER AGE

IN MEMORY OF
PHEBE CHATFIELD
DIED AUGst 26th
1754
IN Ye 18th YEAR
OF HER AGE

Here lies the
Body of Mr Thomas
Davis who Departed
this Life September
the 27th 1751 Aged
65 Years

In Memory
of Benjamin Son
of Mr John & Mrs
Catherine Davis
he died October
ye 19th 1752 in ye 3rd
Year of his Age

In Memory
of Catherine ye
Daughter of Mr
John & Mrs Ca=
therine Davis fhe
died November
3d 1752 in ye 7th year
of her age

In
Memory of
Benjamin Son
to Mr John &
Mrs Catherine
Davis Who
Died July 22
A.D. 1754 Ag-
-ed 9 Weeks

Abigail ye
Daughter of
John & Kathe
rine Davis
died June ye
10th 1758
Aged 9 Weeks
& 3 Days

In Memory of
Iohn Son to
Mr Stephen
& Mrs Amie
Hedges Died
May 2 A D 1759
Aged About
16 years

In Memory of
MR STEPHEN
HEDGES who
died MAY the
2D 1760 Aged
57 Years

In Memory of
John Hedges
Son of Aaron
& Mary Isaacks
who died Novr
14th 1759 Aged
18 Mo & 5 Days

IN MEMORY of
MARY DAUR OF Mr
AARON & Mrs
MARY ISAACS
DIED DECr 21st 1754
AGED 7 WEEKS
& 6 Ds

IN MEMORY of
Katherine ye Wife of
Mr John Davis who
died April 11th A.D.
1759 in ye 37th Year
of her Age
She fear'd the Lord
Obey'd His Voice
Hop'd in His Word
And died of Choice

HERE LYES THE
BODY OF M^{rs}
ELIZABETH GERDINER
THE WIFE OF M^r
JOHN GERDINER
DIED MAY Y^e 19th
1747 IN Y^e 64th
YEAR OF HER AGE

Here lyeth the Body of
Sarah wife of Seth Person^s
Dec^D who dep^D this life
Novr the 8th A.D. 1740
In ye 67th year of her age
Since it so plainly doth appear
We ware not made for to stay here
But that we all muft goe this way
Let us prepare without delay

Here lyes Buried
the Body of
Mr SETH PARSONS
Who Dec^d Sep^t
ye 19th 1725 Aged
about 61 Years

PUAH BARNES DAU^r
TO Mr NOAH & M^{rs}
HANNAH BARNES
DEC^D SEP^{tr} Y^e 14th 1756
IN Y^e 6th YEAR
OF HER AGE

Here lyes Buried
ye Body of M^{rs}
SARAH PARSONS
Who Decr Nov^{br}
ye 15th 1725 Aged
31 Years & 6 M^o

In Memory of
Puah ye wife of
John Davis who
died Decem^r y^e
24th A.D. 1747
in ye 74th Year of
her Age

HERE LYES Y^e BODY
OF Mrs JERUSHA HEDGES
WIDOW OF Mr JEREMIAH
HEDGES AGED 27
YEARS & 9 M^o
DIED MAY Y^e 21st
1742

HERE LYES BURIED
THE BODY OF
LEWIS HEDGES
DEC^D NOV^R 7th
1738
IN Y^e 17th YEAR
OF HIS AGE

HERE LIES BURIED
THE BODY OF M^r
JEREMIAH HEDGES
DEC^D OCTOBER 14th
1738 IN Y^e 25th
YEAR OF HIS AGE

STEPHEN HEDGES.
[This is the footstone. The headstone
is in fragments, the face destroyed, but
was of same size, shape and probable
age, and by the side of that of Jeremiah
Hedges.]

In Memory of
Edward Mulford
who died Sept^r
ye 12th 1754 in y^e
25th Year of
his Age

HERE LYES Y^e BODY
RUTH
OF M^{rs} xxxxxxx CHAMPNEY
WIFE TO Mr SAMUEL
CHAMPNEY AGED 88
YEARS DEC^D APRIL
Y^e 25th 1728

Here Lyes ye Body of
Mr JEREMIAH MILLER
who Decd Janury 2nd
1723/4 Aged 67 Years

Here lyes Buried ye
Body of Mrs MARY
MILLER Widow of Mr
JEREMIAH MILLER
Who Departed this
Life Octr 9th A.D. 1748 in ye
95th Year of Her Age

HERE LYES Ye BODY
OF Mrs MARY MULFORD
WIDOW OF Mr
THOMAS MULFORD
DIED JUNE 14th
1743 in ye 85th
YEAR OF HER AGE

HERE LYES BURIED
THE BODY OF
Mr THOMAS MULFORD
DECD NOVR Ye 2D 1732
IN Ye 77th YEAR
OF HIS AGE

HERE LYES BURIED
THE BODY OF Mrs
MERCY MULFORD WIFE
TO Mr THOs MULFORD
AGED 51 YEARS
DIED MAY Ye 17th
1737

HERE LYETH THE BODY OF DAVID MOLFORD SON OF THOMAS
MOLFORD DEPARTED THIS LIFE SEPR Ye · 12 · 1722 AGED · 22 · YEARS
NINE MONTHS AND 28 DAYS
Ebenezer Mulford Son of Mr Timothy & Mrs Sarah Mulford Decd Janry 8th 1724
Aged 6 weeks.
ESTHER DAUGHTR OF TIMOTHY AND SARAH MULFORD AGED 5
YEARS 5 MO & 7 DS DIED MAY Ye 27th 1717.
Chriftopher Mulford Son of Mr Timothy & Mrs Sarah Mulford Decd Octobr ye
13th 1719 Aged 7 Weeks.
Sarah Daughr of Mr Timothy & Mrs Sarah Mulford Died Sept 14th 1728 Aged 4
weeks.
In Memory of Nathan ye Son of Edward & Amie Mulford who died Decembr 15th
1752 Aged about 2 Months

Here lyes Buried
ye Body of Mr
TIMOTHY MULFORD
Who Departed this
life Decembr 10th Anno
Domi 1741 Aged
about 60 Years

In Memory of
Samvel Parsons
Junr who died
Augft 17th 1752
in ye 59th Year
of his Age

Here lies
the Body of Mrs
Puah Hudfon wife
of Mr Henery
Hudfon who died
July ye 26th 1752 in ye
52nd year of her Age

In Memory
of Mrs Cathe=
rine Relect
to Mr Eanos
Talmage
Who Died
May 12 A.D.
1752 Aged

IN MEMORY of
MEHETABEL the
Daughter of NATHAN
and HANNAH
HEDGES who died
Sept. 28th A.D. 1768
in the 31ft Year
of her Age

In
Memory of Ste-
phen Son to Mr
Recompence &
Mrs Puah Sherrill
Died Auguft 29
A.D. 1757 Aged
6 years

In Memory
of Temperance
the Daughter of
Mr Daniel & Mrs
Rachel Edwards
who died March
ye 7th 1752 in ye 16th
year of her Age

HERE LYETH THE
BODY OF DANIEL

WHO
DEPARTED
THIS LIFE
APRIL 27th
1723

BUSNELL
ÆTATIS
SUÆ

HERE LYETH Ye BODY
OF JOHN CHRISTOPHERS
OF NEW LONDON WHO
IN COMING FROM THE WEST
INDIAS WAS CAST AWAY
ON Ye SOVTH SIDE IN A STORM
IVLY THE 29TH 1723 AND
ALL WERE LOST Ye NEXT
DAY HE WAS DECENTLY
INTERED AGED 22 YEARS

In Memory
of Robert Son of
Mr Robert & Mrs
Mary Parsons
he died Novembr
ye 23rd A.D. 1753 in
ye 9th year of his Age

Here lyes the
Body of Mrs
Lois Hedges Wife
to Mr Samuel
Hedges Who Decd
November 2nd 1718
Aged 38 Years

Heare lies
THE Body of mrs
Sarah Sheriel the wife of
Recompense Sheriel Mr
who died nobr ye 5th Ano. Do
mini 1738 Aged 27
yeares

Puah Daughter
of Recompence
Sherell Died
Augft the 6th
1747 one Year
and 5 months &
18 day

Abraham
Son of Mr
Recompence and
Mrs Puah Sherill
he died March ye
29 1750 in the 4th
year of her age

In Memory
of Jemima Daughtr
of Mr William &
Mrs Jemima Barns
who died Novr
ye 29th 1752 in ye 3d
year of her Age

IN MEMORY of
Capt
JAMES BARNEBY
who died July
the 31th A.D. 1769
in the 39th Year of
his Age

Here lies Interr'd
the Body of Mr
Seth Parfons he
died Auguft ye
22nd A.D. 1752.
being in ye 57th
year of his Age

Here lies the
Body of Mary
Parfons who
Departed this
life May ye 13th
1754 in ye 23d
year of her
Age.

Here lyes ye
Body of Phebe
ye Daughte of
David & Phebe
Mulford Aged
2 months 1753

In Memory of
ABIGAIL MULFORD
the Wife of
JEREMIAH MULFORD
who died MAY 9th
1764 in the 75th
Year of her Age

IN MEMORY of
MEHITABEL Wife
of JESSE DAYTON
she died June the
11th A.D. 1769 in the 33d
Year of her Age

HERE LYES Ye BODY
OF Mrs MARY MULFORD
DAUGHTER OF Mr
JEREMIAH & Mrs
ABIGAIL MULFORD
DIED JANry Ye 25th
1745/6 IN Ye 21ST
YEAR OF HER AGE

In Memory of
Keziah ye Wife of
Jeremiah Sherril
who died Decemr
ye 29th 1750 in ye
22d Year of
her Age

IN MEMORY of
Mr JEREMIAH
MULFORD who
died Octr ye 5th
1766 in ye 76 9th
Year of his Age

Luis ye Son
of Chriftopher
& Elizabeth
Dibble died
Octor 18th 1763
Aged 2 Years
1 Mo & 14 Days

In Memory of
Mrs Ruth Relic
to Deacon Jofiah
Steevens Died
Janua 7 A.D. 1759
in her 79 year

In Memory
of Elias Leek
Son of Mr
Benjamin & Mrs
Charity Leek he
died June the 12th
1753 in the 8th year
of his Age

In Memory of
Mr RECOMPENCE
Sherril who died
Febry 8th 1786
in the 79th year
of his Age

In Memory of
Mrs Joanna Mul-
ford Confort of Mr
Elifha Mulford
who died
of a Cancer
Septr 4th 1791
in the 72d year
of her age

In Memory of
Mr Stephen Sherril
who was drowned
June 22d 1788
in the 30th year
of his Age

IN MEMORY of
Mr THOMAS
MULFORD who
died March 8th
A.D. 1765 in the
77th Year of his Age

In Memory of
Mr.
Elifha Mulford
who departed
this life
May 29th 1798
aged 85 years
4 mo. & 17 days

Here lies the Remains of
Mr SAMUEL BUELL Junr
' Son of the Revd
SAMUEL BUELL &
Mrs MARY BUELL
He departed this Life
Febry 7th 1787 in the
16th year of his Age

David ye Son
of Jeremiah &
Elizabeth Miller
died Augft ye 31st
1752 Aged
14 Days

Samuel ye Son
of Burnit
Miller Efqr
& Elizabeth
his Wife
died Jany
1762 Aged
7 Weeks

Mary Daughter
of Elifha & Eliz
abeth Jones
died Decemr 24th
1751 in ye 4th
Year of her Age

In Memory of
Phebe ye Wife of
Nathan Conkling
who died Febry
ye 5th A.D. 1756
in ye 44th Year
of her Age

Jofiah Son of
John & Phebe
Parfons died
Septr 1st 1752
aged 3 Years
7 Mo & 27 Days

In Memory of
Mrs MARY BUELL
Confort of the
Revd SAMUEL BUELL
who departed this
life May 13th 1783
in the 47th year
of her Age

In Memory of
HENRY Son of
JOSEPH and
PHEBE TILLIN
GHAST died
May 2d 1775
aged 9 Mo and
2 days

Jerufha Daughter
of Jeremiah &
Elizabeth Miller
died Octobr ye 31st
1751 in ye 5th year
of her Age

Elizabeth ye
Daughter of
Elifha & Eliz
abeth Jones
died Decemr
ye 26th 1751 in
ye 2d Year of
her Age

IN MEMORY
of Captn Elifha
Jones who departed
this Life May 18th
A.D. 1764 in the
48th Year of his Age

HERE LYES THE
BODY OF PHEBE
MULFORD AGED
8 YEARS &
11 MONTHS DECD
MARCH THE 21st
1723

Elias ye Son
of Ezekiel &
Elizabeth
Hedges died
April 17th 1755
Aged 3 Weeks
& 5 Days

Mr SAMUEL DAYTON
1745/6
[Footstone; the headstone is missing.]

CORRIGENDA.

A comparison of the foregoing printed sheets of the epitaphs in the old ground at Easthampton with the stones,—made in October, 1900,—requires the following corrections and additions.

MARY CONKLING, p. 55, last line should read "AGED 89 YEARS."
TEMPERANCE HEDGES, p. 57, add completing line "11 MONTHS & 25 Dˢ."
JOSIAH MILLER, p. 58, date "1773" may be "1793."
JOSIAH HEDGES, son of Daniel, p. 58, died "May yᵉ 21ˢᵗ."
MARY MILLER, p. 60, add at bottom "J. Stevens," engraver's name.
NATH'L GARDINER, p. 61, change date of death "1801" to "1804."
ELIZABETH GARDINER, wife of Nathaniel, p. 61, change "Æ. 44" to "Æ. 41."*
LION GARDNER, p. 63, should read "LION GARDINER."
JAIN DAYTON, p. 64, last line should read "Aged 76 years."
MARY HUNTTING, wife of Rev. Nath'l, p. 64, last four lines to be,—

> OF EASTHAMPTON
> WHO DIED OCTᴿ 7ᵗʰ
> 1733 AGED 54
> YEARS & About 5 Mᵒ

JANE OSBORN, p. 67, change date of death to "March the 18ᵗʰ."
DANIEL DAYTON, p. 68, change date of death to "Sepʳ yᵉ 14ᵗʰ."
THOMAS OSBORN, son of Cornelius, p. 68, add two lines to complete,—

> aged 1 month &
> 4 days.

HANNAH BARNS, p. 69, insert in place of the line in brackets,—

> In Memory of
> *Mrs. Hannah Barns*
> Wife of
> *Mr. Noah Barns*
> who died
> Auguſt 8ᵗʰ 1775
> aged 74 years

PUAH BARNES, p. 73, change date of death to "1736."
CATHERINE TALMAGE, p. 74, add completing line "66 years."
MEHETABEL HEDGES. p. 75, should read "Daughter of JONATHAN."
SARAH SHERIEL, p. 75, concluding word of fourth line, though very indistinct, is probably "inʳ" not "Mʳ."
PUAH SHERELL, p. 75, last line should be "18 days old."

* See "Lion Gardiner and his Descendants," by Curtiss C. Gardiner, St. Louis, 1890.

EASTHAMPTON.—North Ground.

At the northerly end of the main street in the village of Easthampton is the Second, or North burying ground, neither as of such ancient date, nor as large as the preceding. All of the inscriptions that were there in 1887 and antedating 1800 are here given.

In Memory of
Uriah Miller
who died
March 15th 1797
in the 77th year
of his age

In Memory of
Samuel Stratton
Son of Mr.
Matthew & Mrs.
Phebe Stratton
who died
Sept. 3d 1784
in the 14th year
of his age

In Memory of
Polly wife of
David Talmage 3d
who died
Auguſt 8th 1796
aged 31 years
and 1 day

In Memory of
Mr. Ellſha Davis,
who departed
this life
April 13th 1792
aged about 80
years

In Memory of
Mrs. Puah Wife of
Mr. Recompenc
Sherril who died
June 18th 1798
in the 83d year
of her age

In Memory of
Mr. John Davis
who died Decr 15th
1798, in the 76th year
of his age
Death was commiſsion'd by
my God,
To take my life away,
And I am here confined to riſe
no more,
Till the great judgment day,
Then with his voice he'll burſt
these bands
And call me to his throne,
To dwell with him eternally,
And his beloved Son.

In
Memory of
Nathan Conklin
who died
Decr 29, 1788
in the 53 year
of his age

In
Memory of
Mehetabel, wife of
Nathan Conklin
who died
March 26, 1784,
aged 44 years.

In Memory of M^r
Jeremiah Mulford
Eldeſt Son of
Mr Ezekiel &
Mrs Amy Mulford
who died Augt 29th
1 7 8 4
in the 23^d year
of his age

In Memory of
Mifs Sarah Conkling
daughter of M^r
Mulford & M^{rs}
Puah Conkling
who died Octr 15th
1780 in the 20th
year of her Age.

In Memory of
Mr Benjamin
Stratton who died
June 27th 1781
in the 35th year
of his Age

IN MEMORY of
Mr WILLIAM
OSBORN who
died January 16th
A.D. 1774 in the
87th Year of his Age

IN MEMORY of Capt
Nathaniel Hunting A.M.
Who Departed this
Life July ye 18th A.D. 1770
in the 68th Year
of his Age

In Memory of
Mrs Mary Hunting
Wife of M^r
Nathan^l Hunting
who died June 5th
1779 in the 45th
Year of her Age

In Memory of
Mrs Mary Hunting
Wife of Capt
Nathaniel Hunting
who died Aug^{ft} 14th
1785 in the 75th
Year of her Age

Jonathan Son
of Mr Jofeph &
Sarah Hunting
who died Octo^r
23^d 1771 Aged
8 M^o & 21 Days

In Memory of
Mr. Lemuel
Mulford who died
Octr 26th 1791,
in the 75th Year
of his Age

In Memory of
Deacon JOHN
GARDINER died
November 24th
1780
in the 59th Year
of
his Age

In Memory of
Mrs ELIZABETH
Wife of Deacon
JOHN GARDINER
died June 16th
1780
in the 56th Year
of her Age

In Memory of
Mrs Elizabeth Miller
Wife of M^r
Timothy Miller
who died July 17
in the year of our
Lord 1786
in the 40th year
of his age.

In Memory of
M^r
Abraham Mulford
who departed this
Life April 12th 1789
in the 71^{ft} Year
of his age

In Memory of
Mr Aaron Fithian
who died Feb^{ry} 2^d
1 7 7 9
Aged 27 years

HERE lies interr'd
what was Mortal of
*Cap*ⁿ Nathan Dayton
who departed this
Life Feby the 14th
Anno : Domini 1773
In the 45th Year of
his Age

In
Memory of
JERUSHA
Daughter of
JONATHAN and
JERUSHA FITHIAN
who died
Septr 25th 1795
aged 3 years
and 7 mo.

In Memory of
Mr Samuel Parfons
who departed
this Life Octo^r 1^{ft}
1790 in the 66th
Year of his Age

In Memory of
Mrs. ABIGAIL CONKLIN,
Wife of
Mr. DANIEL CONKLIN,
who died
Auguft 29th 1784,
in the 45th year
of his age

In Memory af
Mrs. Abiah Mulford
Relict of Mr.
Lemuel Mulford
who died
Feb^{ry} 8th 1793
in the 76th Year
of her Age

In Memory of
Mrs Mary Fithian
who died July 23
1 7 8 0
in the 21st year
of her Age

In Memory of
MARY
Wife of JEREMIAH
GARDINER
who departed this
Life Jan^{ry} the 21^{ft} A.D.
1771 in the 42^d Year
of her Age

IN
Memory of
KEZIA Daughter
of W^m & Elizabeth
Loper who died
Octr 12th 1798
in the 20th year
of her age
Come read my date and here
you'll fee
No age nor fex from death
is free.

In Memory of
MARY Wife of
Samuel Parfons
who died
April 17, 1799
in the 75 year
of her age

Ruth Daughter of
Samuel & Abigail
Baker died April 22^d
A.D. 1775, aged
7 Years & 7 Months

In Memory of
MARY
Wife of JEREMIAH
GARDINER
who departed this
Life Jan^ry the 21^ft A.D.
1771 in the 42^d Year
of her Age.

In
Memory of
PHEBE BAKER
Daughter of
ABRAHAM &
ELIZABETH
BAKER who
died [scaled off]

In Memory of
M^r
Samuel Baker
who died Octr 5th
1786
in the 54th Year
of his Age

In Memory of
Mr. John Parfons
who died
Novr 5th 1775
aged 58 years
and 4 months

Ifaac Son of
Christopher
& Elizabeth
Dibble who
died March 6th
A.D. 1770
Aged 5 Year
& 17 Days

In Memory of
Mrs Mary Baker
Wife of M^r
Abraham Baker
who died April 9
1787
in the 23^d year
of her Age

In Memory of
Mrs Phebe
the wife of M^r
John Parfons
the 4th who died
May 17th 1781
in the 63^d year
of her Age

In Memory of
Mrs Janey Baker
Wife of Lieu^t
Thomas Baker
who died Feb^ry 1^ft
1780 in the 38th
Year of his Age

IN MEMORY of
Henry the only Son
of Mr John Parfons
and Phebe his Wife
who died Janr^y 1^ft
1771 in ye 29th Year
of his Age

Behold Infcrib'd upon this Stone
A Blooming Youth an only Son
His Father's Groan nor Mother's Cries
Could not avail Lo here He Lies

,In Memory of
Dr. SAMUEL HUTCH-
INSON who died
March 4th 1790
in the 57th year
of his age

In Memory of
PHEBE Wife of
Dr. SAMUEL HUTCH-
ENSON who died
May 6th 1784
in the 40th year
of her age

83

IN MEMORY of
SARAH Wife of
JACOB WICKHAM
who died June the
20th A.D. 1770 in the
62d Year of her Age

In Memory of
Mr Jacob Wickham
who departed this
Life July 8, 1776
in the 73d Year of
his Age

In Memory of Mrs
Abigail Conkling
wife of Capt. Jeremiah
Conkling who Died
June 16 AD 1780 in the
58th year of her age
My Flefh fhall flumber in the ground
Till the laft Trumpet's Joyful found
Then burft the Chains with fweet furprife
And in my Saviour's image rife.

EARLY EASTHAMPTON WILLS.

Abstracts from New York Surrogate's Office.

By Orville B. Ackerly, Esq.

Mary Gardiner (Lib. 1, 6), will of Apr. 19, 1664, widow of Lion, of Maidstone, als. Easthampton; son David, dau. Mary Conckling, gr. child Elizabeth Howell, son in law Jeremiah Conckling, son in law Arthur Howell; servants (slaves) Japhet and Boose; overseers to be Rev. Thomas James, John Mulford and Robert Boud; executor son David; codicil dated Jan. 15, 1664-5; probated June 6, 1665.

William Fithian (Lib. 2, 270), will of Dec. 11, 1678, wife Margaret; sons Enoch and Samuel; daus. Sarah and Hannah; grand child, dau. of dec'd dau. Martha; son Sam'l to be ex'r after his mother's decease; Thomas Baker and Thomas James overseers; probated March, 1679.

Nathaniel Sylvester (Lib. 7, 206), will of Ap. 3, 1700, wife Margaret, dau. of Capt. Josiah Hobart of Easthampton; sons Nathaniel and Brinley; daus. Margaret and Grizzell; William Nicoll and Col. Henry Pierson ex'rs. Codicil of Ap. 24, 1705, testator now of Newport, R. I., Benj. Newberry and Arnold Collins to succeed Col. Pierson, dec'd, as ex'rs. Second codicil, not dated, confirms. All probated at Newport, July 4, 1705, Nicoll qualifying ex'r.

Richard Shaw (Lib. 7, 409), will of Oct. 7, 1708, wife Rebecca, sons John and Richard both under 21; four daus. not named; wife sole ex'r; probated May 6, 1709.

Robert Daiton (Lib. 8, 137), will of Feb. 11, 1710-11, wife, sons Samuel and Beriah, gr. sons Robert Daiton and John Daiton under 21; sons Beriah and Samuel ex'rs. Codicil of Ap. 14, 1712, names gr. child Mary Terril and dau. Alce Edwards. Probated June 14, 1712.

Abraham Schellenx (Lib. 8, 221), will of Mar. 7, 1709-10, sons William (the eldest), Abraham, Isaac and Zachariah; daus. Johannah (already married), Rachel and Anne; land in Westchester co. bought of Robert Walters Ap. 6, 1705; Capt. Abraham Howell, Capt. Theophilus Howell, Ebenezer White, Capt. Thomas Chatfield, William Schellenx and Isaac Hedges ex'rs; probated Mar. 27, 1712.

Jacob Scelinx (Lib. 8, 322), will of Jan. 8, 1712, wife Hannah, sons Jacob, Daniel, Jonathan, all under 21; five daus. not named; requests brother Nath'l Baker, his son Jonathan Baker, and Ananias Conkling to be overseers; probated Ap. 11, 1714. Letters of admin'n granted to widow.

Samuel Parsons (Lib. 8, 398), aged and infirm, will of May 6, 1709, wife Hannah, son Seth, gr. ch. Henry Parsons; son Seth sole ex'r; probated Mar. 30, 1716.

Josiah Edwards (Lib. 9, 246), will of Feb. 9, 1712-13, husbandman, sons Josiah, Joseph, Churchill, Jonathan, David and Nathaniel, all under 21; wife, not named; daus. Martha, Mercy and Mary all under 18; Ananias Conkling, Lewis Conkling and brother Thomas Edwards, ex'rs; probated Aug. 8, 1721.

James Dyment (Lib. 9, 344), will of Aug. 24, 1721, wife Elizabeth, sons Thomas (eldest), John and Nathaniel; daus. Hannah Moore and Abigail Lubtan(?); gr. dau. Hannah Hoping; sons John and Nathan'l ex'rs; probated March 9, 1722.

Joseph Stretton (Lib. 9, 391), will of Oct. 8, 1722, yeoman, wife Sarah, daus. Hannah Gessop and Martha, wife of Ananias Conkling; gr. children Joseph, Margaret and Mary, children of Ananias Conkling; by ante-nuptial agreement between testator and wife dated Oct. 28, 1714, she agrees to accept £20, he now gives her £10 more; son-in-law Ananias Conkling and John Davis ex'rs; probated Mar. 29, 1723.

ONESSIMUS TALMAGE (Lib. 9, 394), will of Jan. 31, 1722-3, sick, wife Rebeckah; daus. Phebe Gold, Sarah and Mary unm.; Edward Jones, Jr., and bro-in-law John Wheeler ex'rs: pro. March 9, 1723.

MICAH BAKER (Lib. 9, 463), will of Sep. 25, 1723, farmer, wife Elizabeth. " in case I have a son * * * in case I should have two daughters"; Nath'l Baker and Samuel Baker ex'rs; pro. Ap. 2, 1725.

SAMUEL MULFORD (Lib. 10, 81), will of Ap. 16, 1725, merchant, wife not named with whom there is an ante-nuptial agreement; sons Samuel, Timothy, Elias and Matthew, the last to be ex'r.; pro. Sep. 30, 1725.

ROBERT HUDSON (Lib. 10, 229), will of Ap. 26, 1723, blacksmith, wife Mary, sons Samuel, Henry, and John, and seven other children, not named, all under 21; wife to be ex'x, assisted by son Samuel and Thomas Chatfield; pro. Apr. 2, 1724.

JOHN MULFORD, Jr. (Lib. 10, 308), yeoman, sick, will of Jan. 5, 1726-7. wife Hannah, sons John and Josiah, sisters Jane and Deborah, dau. Phebe under 18; bro-in-law Theophilus Pierson of Bridgehampton, and wife ex'rs; pro. Mar. 31, 1727.

JOHN EDWARDS (Lib. 11, 42), yeoman, will of Aug. 31, 1728. wife Ann executrix); daus. Anne King, Elishabah Frances, Phebe, Esther, Jerusha and Elizabeth; sons Timothy, Henry and John, under 21; pro. June 13, 1730.

THOMAS MULFORD (Lib. 11, 511), yeoman, will of Feb. 14, 1726-7, wife Mary; sons Thomas, William, Ezekiel, Lewis and Jeremiah; daus. Rachel Debett and Abiah Hedges; son Ezekiel's three ch.; son Lewis's two ch.; gr. son Lewis Mulford, gr. dau. Jane, dau. of Lewis Mulford, under 18; sons Thomas and Jeremiah ex'rs; pro. Feb. 14, 1732.

EBENEZER LEEK (Lib. 12, 186), will of Mar. 19, 1722-3, wife Hannah. sons Recompense, Stephen and Ichabod; daus. Hannah Allen, Aylce Smith and Abigail Woodruffe; son Recompense ex'r; pro. July 3, 1734.

JEREMIAH CONCKLING (Lib. 12, 228), yeoman, will of Jan. 11, 1732-3. nephew Elisha, son of bro. Cornelius, niece Jane, dau. of Samuel Conkling dec'd. under 18; adopted son Jeremiah, natural son of said Elisha, under 21; wife Jane and Kinsman Elisha Conckling ex'rs; pro. Aug. 26, 1734.

THOMAS BAKER (Lib. 12, 400), will of Feb. 11, 1721, wife Elizabeth. dau. Mercy under 18; sons Thomas, Daniel, Micah, Samuel, Jeremiah, John and Nathaniel; son Nath'l ex'r; pro. Dec. 4, 1735.

DAVID CONKLING (Lib. 13, 261), will of Dec. 20, 18th y'r of George II. gr. son Jeremiah Conkling under 21, son David, dau. Jane, other daus. not named; son David ex'r; pro. Mar. 8, 1738.

NATHANIEL BAKER (Lib. 13, 263), yeoman, will of Ap. 12, 1738; sons Jonathan and Daniel; daus. Abigail Hedges, Catterina Mulford, Hannah Parsons, Johannah Ogden and Mary Woodruff; gr. dau. Cattarina Woodruff, son-in-law Samuel Parsons, gr. dau. Mary Woodruff; son Daniel and neighbor Thomas Osborne, Jr. ex'rs; pro. March 8, 1738.

JOHN GARDINER (Lib. 13, 297), gentleman, will of Dec. 14, 1737, wife Elizabeth, dau. Hannah Chandler, dau. Elizabeth Green, son Joseph, dau. Sarah Trente, gr. dau. Dorothy Trente under 18, gr. dau. Sarah Trente, gr. son Jonathan Trente under 21; Elizabeth and Jerusha, daus. of dec'd son John, under 18; Samuel and John Gray, sons of dec'd dau. Mary Gray, under 21; Elizabeth dau. of dec'd son Samuel; gr. dau. Sarah Chandler under 18; Jonathan son of dec'd son Jonathan, under 21; son David, friend Nathaniel Huntting, nephews Lion and Giles Gardiner, Samuel, son of dec'd son Samuel, son Joseph; Nath'l Huntting, Jr. and William Hedges, Jr. ex'rs; pro. Aug. 1, 1738.

JOHN HEDGES (Lib. 13, 311), yeoman, will of Jan. 31, 1733-4, wife Ruth, sons John, Stephen and Lemuel; some "meadow that was father Stratton's"; dau. Ruth; sons John and Stephen ex'rs; pro. Ap. 27, 1737.

THOMAS EDWARDS (Lib. 13, 316), yeoman, will of Oct. 18, 1736, wife Mary, sons John, James, David and Daniel, gr. son Jacob Edwards, daus. Sarah, Mary and Hannah; sons David and Daniel ex'rs; pro. July 11, 1737.

DANIEL BAKER (Lib. 13, 430), will of May 15, 1740, wife Abigail, son Daniel, brother Jonathan, son Abraham under 21, sons Nathaniel and Henry; land in Elizabethtown in E. Jersey; three daus. not named; friend Eleazar Miller and brother Thomas Ozburn ex'rs; pro. Aug. 26, 1740.

ANNANIAS CONCKLING (Lib. 13, 434), yeoman, will of Apr. 11, 1739, wife Hannah, sons Annanias, Henry, Lemuel, Nathan, Benjamin, Daniel and Josiah; daus. Bethiah Hicks and Hannah Barnes; son Nathan ex'r; pro. Aug. 26, 1740.

JANE CONCKLING (Lib. 14, 101), will of Apr. 11, 1738, three sisters Sarah Leek, Deborah Parsons and Hannah Conkling; two cows to Jeremiah Conkling, the natural son of Jane Gardiner, wife of Giles Gardiner; Jane Conckling, dau. of Samuel Conckling, dec'd; Clemens Huntting residuary legatee; friends John Hunting and Clemens, his present wife, ex'rs; pro. May 29, 1714.

TIMOTHY MULFORD (Lib. 14, 267), yeoman, will of Dec. 9, 1741, wife Sarah, sons Timothy, Christopher (under 21) and Edward; bro. Samuel; dau. Amy; son Timothy ex'r; pro. Feb. 24, 1742.

ROBERT PARSONS (Lib. 15, 30), will of Sep. 1, 1717, wife Mary, sons Robert, John (both under 21); bro. Samuel, bro.-in-law Nath'l Demony and friend John Davis overseers; wife sole ex'x; pro. Dec. 20, 1742.

EDWARD HUNTTING (Lib. 15, 415), doctor, will of Mar. 19, 1744-5, wife Mercy, sons Isaac Mulford and Edward, both under 21, daus. Mercy, Mehitable and Mary, under 18; wife, her father, Isaac Mulford, and bro. Samuel Huntting, ex'rs; pro. Apr. 24, 1745.

MATHIAS BURNET (Lib. 15, 549), will of July 20, 1745, wife Elizabeth, gr. son Burnett, four gr. sons Jeremiah, Eleazer, Annanias and Abraham; four gr. daus. not named, son in law not named; gr. son Burnet sole ex'r; pro. Apr. 3, 1746.

SAMUEL DAYTON (Lib. 15, 590), yeoman, will of Nov. 2, 1739, wife Dorithy, gr. son Henry Dayton, son of Daniel; father Robert Dayton; son Jonathan, son-in-law William Osborn, and Osborn's dau. Joanah Mulford; dau. Elizabeth Osborn; four youngest ch. of dau. Joanah Serle; sons Daniel and Nathan ex'rs; pro. Apr. 3, 1746.

BERIAH DAYTON (Lib. 16, 31), of Pantico, will of Apr. 18, 1746, wife Jane, sons Jeremiah, John and Beriah; apprentice John Fields; daus. Rachel Dymont, Martha Brown, Esther Brown, Marah Conkling and Jane Dayton; sons John and Jeremiah ex'rs; pro. Sep. 19, 1746.

JOSEPH OSBURNE, Jr. (Lib. 16, 44), will of Apr. 6, 1739, wife Mary, sons Thomas, Jeremiah and Joseph; dau. Mary Baker, bro. Daniel; had tanyard and bark mill; sons Jeremiah and Joseph ex'rs; pro. Sep. 19, 1746.

JOHN CONKLING (Lib. 16, 47), will of Jan. 3, 1739, sons John, Elias and Jonathan; Elias ex'r; pro. Aug. 23, 1746.

CHARLES BORTNER (Lib. 16, 187) of Berlin in Prussia, now of E., physician and chirurgeon, will of May 3, 1747, watch, gold buttons and knee buckles to Thomas Talmage; diamond ring to Hezekiah Usher; gold clasps to John Mackie; two gold rings to Elizabeth Hedges; walking cane to Jonathan Huntting; snuff-box to Mrs. Joseph Havens, and " saphier stone in the shape of a cane head " to his ex'rs to sell, the proceeds to be put at interest for the maintenance of a school in E.; surgical instruments to John Mackie with his wearing apparel, and his man saddle and bridle to Thomas Talmage and his wife and their son Thomas; friends Jonathan Huntting of E., and John Mackie of Southampton ex'rs; pro. June 8, 1747.

JONATHAN BAKER (Lib. 16, 326), carpenter, will of May 31, 1743, wife Hannah, son Jonathan, gr. son Jacob Baker; wife and son ex'rs; pro. Sept. 12, 1748.

ARON FITHIAN (Lib. 17, 289), yeoman, will of Jan. 12, 1750, weak, wife Bettiah, daus. Mary Talmage and Ester Jones, son David; wife and friend Eliezer Miller ex'rs; pro. June 28, 1750.

JONATHAN HUNTTING (Lib. 17, 391), shopkeeper, will of Jan. 7, 1750, wife Esther, children (not named); wife and her father Mathew Mulford ex'rs; pro. May 8, 1751.

DAVID GARDINER (Lib. 17, 415), of Isle of Wight, gentleman, will of May 16, 1751, sick, wife Mehetable; Mehetable Burrows and Mary Burrows, his wife's daus; sons John, David, Abraham, and daus. Abigail, and Hannah; sons David and Abraham ex'rs; pro. July 23, 1751.

SETH PARSONS (Lib. 18, 255), yeoman, will of Aug. 12, 1752, sick, wife Abigail, cousin Seth Barnes; nephew Seth Woodruff, son of sister Elizabeth; nephew Recompense Sherrill, son of sister Puah; nephew Seth Parsons, son of brother John; bro.-in-law Recompense Sherrill, Jr., neices Mary and Abigail Parsons, daus. of brother John; wife and bro.-in-law Sherrill ex'rs; pro. Sep. 21, 1752.

MARAH CONCKLING (Lib. 19, 2), widow of Luis Conckling, will of Aug. 15, 1747, son Sineas; four gr. ch. William, Zebedy, Abraham and Elizabeth Pierson;

two gr. ch. Chrysopher and Sineas Dible; three gr. ch. Daniel, Luis and John Miller; daus. now living, Esther, Zeriah and Abigail; son Sineas and. Burnet Miller ex'rs; pro. Jan. 11, 1754.

ELIPHALET STRATTON (Lib. 19, 8), yeoman, will of Mar. 19, 1745, wife Phebe, three youngest daus. Rebecca, Mary and Phebe under 18; dau. Martha Pierson; sons Jeremiah, David, Samuel and Abraham; sons Jeremiah, David, and Samuel when he is 21, to be ex'rs; pro. Jan. 11, 1754.

THOMAS CHATFIELD (Lib. 19. 11), will of May 14, 1751, wife Hannah, son John, gr. son Thomas, son of dec'd son Thomas, " father Stratten; " gr. daus. Phebe and Abigail Chatfield and daus. Mary Gelston and Anna Mulford; three ch. of dec'd son Thomas; pro. Jan. 23, 1754.

NATHANIEL HUNTING (Lib. 19, 14), clark, will of Sept. 17, 1751, sons Nathaniel, Samuel and John: two gr. sons ch. of dec'd son Edward, Isaac and Edward; also Edward's two daus. Mercy and Mehitable; gr. sons Jonathan and Matthew, ch. of dec'd son Jonathan; gr. son Nathaniel; sons John and Samuel ex'rs; pro. Feb. 11, 1754.

THOMAS OSBORN, Jr. (Lib. 19, 23), taylor, will of Nov. 14, 1753, wife Jean (now with child), son Thomas, daus. Deborah, Jean, Mary and Elizabeth; bros. Joseph and Jeremiah Osborn ex'rs; pro. Jan. 11, 1754.

JOSIAH OSBORNE (Lib. 19, 202), will of Sept. 12, 1754, wife, not named; sons Jedediah and Jonathan; daus. Sarah and Zariah Osborne; Daniel Leak and James Hand, Jr. ex'rs; pro. Dec. 10, 1754.

EDWARD MULFORD (Lib. 19, 204), joyner, will of Sept. 7, 1754, wife Amey, son Nathan; wife and bro. Timothy Mulford ex'rs; pro. Dec. 10, 1754.

JOHN HAND (Lib. 19, 335), yeoman, will of Feb. 1, 1755, wife Hannah, sons Daniel, Henry and John; daus. Mary and Phebe; sons John and Daniel ex'rs; pro. Sep. 11, 1755.

JOSEPH HICKS (Lib. 19, 338), yeoman, will of Feb. 28, 1755; wife Bethia, sons Bishop, Joseph and Samuel; daus. Elizabeth, Bethia and Mary; wife and bro.-in-law Nathan Conckling ex'rs; pro. Sep. 26, 1755.

JAMES HAND, Jr. (Lib. 20, 453), will of Oct. 19, 1757, sick, wife Mary, son James, dau. Jemima under 21; wife and Job Pierson ex'rs; pro. Dec. 14, 1757.

DANIEL OSBORN (Lib. 20, 455), tanner, will of Sep. 23, 1750, wife, not named, two daus., sons Daniel, Jonathan and David; gr. father Thomas Osborn dec'd; son Jonathan and cousin Joseph Osborne ex'rs; pro. Jan. 12, 1758.

EPHRAIM BURNET (Lib. 22, 416), cordwainer, will of Feb. 1, 1761; wife, not named, dau. Sybill Cook, son Stephen, gr. son Stephen Burnit; pro. Feb. 9, 1761.

ELISHA OSBORN (Lib. 22, 420), will of Jan. 26, 1761, wife Elizabeth, sons Zebedi, Elisha and Matthew; dau. Ruth Stratton; Elizabeth (relationship not stated); dau. Ester Osborn; Daniel Leek and son Zebedi exrs; pro. Feb. 13, 1761.

WILLIAM CONKLING (Lib. 22, 513), will of Nov. 29, 1760, wife Ruth, dau. Ruth, sons William, Stephen and Abraham, dau. Mary, youngest son Jacob; John Chatfield and son Jacob ex'rs; pro. Mar. 18, 1761.

STEPHEN HEDGES (Lib. 23, 151), yeoman, will of May 22, 1759; wife Annie, sons Matthew, Elias, Timothy and Nathaniel; 40 acres " at a place called Newbourgh on the Hudson River"; daus. Annie, Esther and Ruth; son Nathaniel to be maintained by Matthew and Elias jointly after Elias is 21; Wm. Hedges, Jr. and Timothy Mulford ex'rs; pro. Aug. 27, 1761.

ELIAS MULFORD (Lib. 23, 154), yeoman, will of Apr. 16, 1756, wife Mary, daus. Elizabeth and Phebe, son Samuel; wife and son ex'rs; pro. Oct. 10, 1761.

JAMES HAND (Lib. 23, 156), will of Oct. 19, 1754, sick, wife, not named, sons James, Jr., Ezekiel, Jeremiah and Samuel; daus. Mary Thorps, Sarah Talmage and Rebecca Hand; gr. dau. Experience Hand; son James, and Elenor, son of Elnathan White ex'rs; pro. Oct. 17, 1761.

JONATHAN HEDGES (Lib. 24, 17), will of Dec. 16, 1762, wife Hannah, brother Benjamin, daus. Lois Barnabe, Mehitable and Abigail, sons Reuben and Jonathan; col. Abraham Gardiner and son Jonathan ex'rs; pro. April 16, 1763.

DANIEL DAYTON (Lib. 24, 185), will of Sept. 14, 1761, wife Mary, sons Daniel and Henry, and the latter's three children, Deborah, Hannah and Samuel; dau. Mary Mulford and three of her children, Mary, Jonathan and Nathan; wife and son Daniel ex'rs; prob. May 19, 1763.

NATHAN DAYTON (Lib. 24, 472), will of March 10, 1763, sons Nathan, Abraham and Jonathan (the latter to support his brother Samuel), daus. Elizabeth and Joanna; sons Nathan and Abraham ex'rs; prob. June 30, 1764.

JOHN GARDINER (Lib. 24, 520).*

GILES GARDINER (Lib. 24, 522), will of Jan. 17, 1760, son Abraham Baker, grandson Roscel Gardiner, dau. Elizabeth Baker, grand dau. Abigail Gardiner; Uriah Miller and John Gardiner ex'rs; prob. Nov. 7, 1764.

JOHN TALMAGE (Lib. 24, 524), will of Oct 10, 1760, wife Ann, sons John, Ennis (Enos?), Jeremiah, Daniel, David, Nathaniel and Josiah; Elizabeth Hedges, Experience Edwards, Rebecca Cady, Abigail Conkling and Margaret Butler (probably daughters); three youngest daus. Hannah Leek, Martha Strong and Rachel Talmage; Elihu Howell and Daniel Leek ex'rs; pro. Nov. 7, 1764.

BETHIAH BURNIT (Lib. 24, 527) will of July 25, 1764, son Stephen Burnit, grand daus. Mary Burnit and Sybel Cook; dau. Sybel Cook; son Abraham Cook ex'r; pro. Nov. 9, 1764.

THOMAS MULFORD (Lib. 25, 89), will of May 28, 1757, yeoman, wife Deborah, sons Elisha, Thomas, Daniel and Barnabas; sons Elisha and Thomas ex'rs; pro. June 26, 1765.

JOHN DIMON (Lib. 25, 92), will of March 8, 1764, yeoman, daus. Deborah Miller, Elizabeth Hand, Rachel and Mary; sons John, Abraham and Isaac, the last two ex'rs; pro. June 26, 1765.

JOHN DAVIES (Lib. 25, 292), will of Aug. 30, 1763, aged and infirm, dau. in law Mehittabel Stratton and her son Benjamin Stratton; nephew John Davis; devises to Jonathan Baker, Deborah wife of Josiah Miller, Jr., John Davis Jr., Abigail wife of Daniel Conkling, Hannah wife of Lion Gardiner; books of history and divinity to Mehettable Stratton, Hannah Gardiner, Abigail Conkling and nephew John Davis; Mehittabel Stratton, John Davis, Jr., and friends John Gardiner and Daniel Conkling, ex'rs; pro. Aug. 8, 1766.

JOHN STRATTON (Lib. 25, 461), will of May 7, 1759, farmer. wife Elizabeth, sons Matthew, Stephen, John and Samuel; daus. Hannah, Phebe, Amy and Elizabeth; wife and son Matthew ex'rs; codicil of Aug. 29, 1761; pro. Jan. 28, 1767.

CORNELIUS CONKLING (Lib. 25, 464), will of March 30, 1765, yeoman, dau. in law Ruth, widow of dec'd son Cornelius; gr. son Cornelius under 18, Ruth, Deborah and Abigail, all children of dec'd son Cornelius; daus. Elizabeth and Esther; children of dec'd daus. Mary and Jane; sons Mulford and Nathan, who are ex'rs with friend Eleazer Miller; pro. Jan. 28, 1767.

JEREMIAH MULFORD (Lib. 25, 466), will of Dec. 28, 1765, yeoman, sons Lemuel, Ezekiel, Jeremiah, Job, Abraham and David; daus. Hannah Brant and Abigail Howell; sons Lemuel and Ezekiel ex'rs; pro. Dec. 17, 1766.

DANIEL HAND (Lib. 25, 480), will of Feb. 13, 1761, wife Sarah, sons Josiah, Silas and David; land in Hanover, Morris Co., N. J.; dau. Elizabeth Pierson; wife and son David ex'rs; pro. Mar. 11, 1767.

DAVID CONKLING (Lib. 26, 270), will of Sept 5, 1754, yeoman, indisposed, wife Hannah, sons David and Simon, daus. Hannah Dayton and Sarah Conkling; sons Samuel and Zebulon ex'rs; pro. Dec. 24, 1767.

THOMAS MILLER (Lib. 26, 284), will of Apr. 19, 1766, wife Hannah, son Thomas "if compos mentis when 21," two married daughters, and four younger daughters; friends Job Pierson and Daniel Leek ex'rs with wife; pro. Jan. 12, 1768.

JOHN HUNTTING (Lib. 26, 359), will of Feb. 23, 1768, cooper, wife Clemence, daus. Clemence Sherrell, Jane Conkling, Ruth Miller, Mary Osborn, Phebe Mulford, Lucreshe Miller, Temperance Conkling, Jerusha Hedges and Easter Chatfield; four gr. daus. children of dec'd dau. Elizabeth Miller, Mary, Elizabeth, Phebe and Ruth; dau. in law Jane Conkling; three sons in law, Burnet Miller, Jeremiah Miller and capt. David Mulford ex'rs; prob. Apr. 25, 1768.

ISAAC BARNS (Lib. 27, 156), will of Jan 2, 1765, son Isaac, daus. Patience, Elizabeth and Anna; friends Noah Barns and David Stratton ex'rs; pro. Sept. 16, 1769.

NATHANIEL HUNTTING (Lib. 27, 289), will of July 18, 1768, wife Mary, sons Nathaniel, William and Joseph, grandson John Huntting, three sons ex'rs; pro. July 25, 1770.

* This will is printed in full in "Lion Gardiner and his Descendants," by Curtiss G. Gardiner, St. Louis, 1900.

JONATHAN HEDGES (Lib. 27, 291), will of Oct. 9, 1769, wife and children (not named); wife and friends Timothy Miller and Benjamin Hedges ex'rs; pro. July 25, 1770.

JAMES BARNABY (Lib. 27, 401) will of July 24, 1769, wife Lois, son James, daus. Hannah, Sabra and Elizabeth (speaks of " sons and daughters "); Thomas Wickham and John Chatfield ex'rs; pro. Nov. 26, 1770.

BETHIAH FITHIAN (Lib. 27, 402), will of Mar. 5, 1768, spinster, son David Fithian, " my great bible," " dau. Mary Talmage the child of my dau. Esther Johnes "; John Gardiner and John Davis ex'rs, pro. Nov. 26, 1770.

HENRY CONCKLING (Lib. 27, 403), will of July 7, 1770, yeoman, wife Amy, sons Henry (under 21) and Jedediah, daus. Charlotte, Amy, Mary, Sarah, Cloah, Hannah, Ruth and Easter; wife, brother John Davis and brother Edward Conkling ex'rs; pro. Nov. 26, 1770.

JOSIAH MILLER (Lib. 27, 406), will of Feb. 13, 1768, yeoman, son Josiah; grandson David, son of Josiah; son Jeremiah; dau. Phebe Parsons; son Matthew Miller, "a cripple and unable to support himself"; son in law John Parsons 4th and son Jeremiah ex'rs; pro. Nov. 26, 1770.

TIMOTHY MILLER (Lib. 27, 409), will of Apr. 27, 1769, wife Hannah, sons Daniel, Timothy, Peleg, Elisha and David; daus. Zurviah, Temperance, Elizabeth, Hannah and Charlotte (all Miller); wife, and sons David and Elisha ex'rs; pro. Nov. 26, 1770.

WILLIAM HEDGES (Lib. 27, 582) will of Jan. 28, 1755, yeoman, "poorly in body," sons William and Stephen; grandson David, son of dec'd son Jeremiah; son Ezekiel; five daus. Hannah, Mary, Zurviah, Elizabeth and Phebe; sons William and Stephen ex'rs; pro. Jan. 14, 1771.

NATHANIEL BAKER (Lib. 28, 259) will of Apr. 10, 1771, son (oldest) David, and Samuel ("youngest now living"), daus. Sarah Hedges and Phebe Howet(?); sons ex'rs; pro. June 2, 1772.

NATHAN DAYTON (Lib. 28, 448) will of Feb. 3, 1773, sons Abraham, Elias and Nathan; daus. Amy, Phebe, and Mary; brother Samuel to be maintained by the six children; brother Samuel Mulford and friend Stephen Hedges ex'rs; pro. March 5, 1773.

JEREMIAH TALMAGE (Lib. 28, 452), will of Aug. 29, 1770, farmer, wife Mary, son Jeremiah, wife and loving brother Daniel Leek ex'rs: pro. Mar. 5, 1773.

MATTHEW MULFORD (Lib. 29, 105), will of Apr. 23, 1774, yeoman, grandson David Hedges, granddaus. Elizabeth and Jerusha Gardiner; "lawful" son Daniel Mulford, who is ex'r; pro. June 2, 1774.

DAVID GARDINER (Lib. 29, 188), will of Sept. 7, 1774, gentleman, of the Isle of Wight, wife Jerusha, sister Jerusha Gardiner; brother Septimus, sister Hannah Gardiner, youngest son David, oldest son John Lyon Gardiner; children all under 21; uncles Col. Abraham Gardiner and Capt. David Mulford, and friend Thomas Wickham ex'rs; pro. Sept. 16, 1774.

MARY MILLER (Lib. 30, 68), will of Oct. 15, 1770, wife of Eleazar Miller, cousins Patrick Authur Gold and Sarah Farnon; silver tankard "which was father Howell's" to Annanias Cooper's four daus.; cousin Pheby, wife of Theophilus Halsey; three daus. of James Hildradge, Marah, Rebekah and Pheby, under 18; sons of James Hildrage, Joshua, Noah and David, under 21; to Elisha Pain, pastor of the church at Mecot £4, and £60 for charitable uses; James Hildrage, Jr.; husband signs approval; Elisha Pain, John Cook and Annanias Cooper, all of Southampton, ex'rs; pro. Nov. 28, 1775.

JOHN DAYTON (Lib. 30, 176), will of Mar. 5, 1768, sick, wife Abigail, son John; names wife's first husband Seth Parsons; four daus. Joanna, Elizabeth, Phebe and Martha, grandsons John, Josiah, and David Dayton; wife, son John, and Burnet Miller ex'rs; pro. Apr. 27, 1776.

WILLIAM OSBORN (Lib. 30, 233), will of Jan. 12, 1771, yeoman, wife Sarah, grandson William Mulford, dau. Johannah Mulford; said gr.son and Abraham Gardiner, ex'rs; pro. Feb. 25, 1774.

DAVID BAKER (Lib. 30, 249), will of Apr. 1, 1774, yeoman, wife Mehitable, daus. Mary and Sarah, son David under 20; "cane, sword, desk and plate that was my father's"; wife and brothers in law Abraham Miller and Stephen Hedges, ex'rs; pro. April 19, 1774.

ABRAHAM GARDINER, Esq. (Lib. 35, 205), will of Aug. 18, 1772, indisposed, wife Mary, sons Abraham and Nathaniel, daus. Mary Thomson and Rachel Mulford; friend and niece Ruth Smith; friend Rev. Samuel Buell, M.A.; wife and two sons and sons in law Isaac Thomson and David Mulford ex'rs; pro. Dec. 30, 1782.

PHEBE PARSONS (Lib. 37, 74), will of May 17, 1781, very sick, dau. Phebe, gr. daus. Phebe and Elizabeth, cousin Lucretia Wickham, dau. Mary Osborn; "the noat that I have against Jeremiah"; friend Stephen Hedges and son Jeremiah Osborn ex'rs; pro. May 10, 1784.

JONATHAN OSBORN (Lib. 37, 75), will of Nov. 11, 1781, yeoman, wife Elizabeth, son Joseph, brother David, youngest son Daniel, sons Jonathan, Henry and Samuel; Samuel Hutchinson, sons Joseph and Jonathan ex'rs; pro. May 19, 1784.

JOHN PARSONS 4th (Lib. 37, 78), will of Oct. 21, 1775, yeoman, indisposed, wife Phebe, daus. Phebe Hutchinson and Mary Parsons, son in law Samuel Hutchinson; wife, son in law, and dau. Mary ex'rs; pro. May 19, 1784.

WILLIAM JAGGER (Lib. 37, 83), will of July 25, 1775, mariner; wife Abigail sole devisee and ex'x; pro. May 19, 1784.

ELIAS CONKLING (Lib. 38, 73), will of May 29, 1780, wife (unnamed), daus. Loes, Mary and Amey; wife and Ezekiel Mulford ex'rs; pro. June 20, 1785.

ZEBADEE OSBORN (Lib. 38, 371), will of Dec. 2, 1785, yeoman, wife Mary, dau. Abigail Norris, sons Abraham and Elisha; brother Elisha and son Elisha ex'rs; pro. Dec. 22, 1785.

JOHN MULFORD (Lib. 38, 373), will of Aug. 23, 1783, yeoman, sick, only son Josiah, wife (not named); gr. son John, eldest son of dec'd son John; daus. Jerusha, Esther and Mary; gr. dau. Phebe, child of dec'd dau. Hannah; brothers in law John Dayton and Abraham Miller, and son Josiah ex'rs; pro. Jan. 26, 1786.

RECOMPENSE SHERRILL (Lib. 39, 4), will of Feb. 4, 1786, yeoman, sons Abraham and Stephen, eldest son Recompense, eldest dau. Sarah Conkling, dau. Puah, unmarried; wife (not named); sons Abraham and Stephen, and doctor Samuel Hutchinson ex'rs; pro. Mar. 14, 1786.

JOHN HEDGES (Lib. 39, 5), will of Mar. 10, 1786, yeoman, daus. Mary Isaacs and Ruth Howell; son Daniel and Jeremiah Miller ex'rs; pro. Mar. 14, 1786.

MULFORD CONKLING (Lib. 39, 13), will of Jan. 23, 1781, yeoman, son Daniel (under 21), wife Puah, daus. Puah and Mary, son Mulford; wife, bro. Nathan Conkling Jr. and Jesse Dayton, ex'rs; pro. Mar. 27, 1786.

JEDEDIAH OSBORNE (Lib. 39, 67), will of Feb. 19, 1785, very weak, sons Jacob, John and Isaac, and "other children"; "Jacob to improve his land until son Isaac shall return home"; sons Jacob and Isaac ex'rs, (only Jacob qualified); pro. Apr. 18, 1786.

SAMUEL BAKER (Lib. 39, 302), will of Feb. 25, 1786, yeoman, wife Abigail, son Thomas, daus. Joanne, Amy, Sarah and Hannah; sons Nathaniel, Lewis and Abraham; bro. David dec'd; wife and Nathaniel Dominy ex'rs; pro. Oct. 20, 1786.

WILLIAM SCHELLINX (Lib. 9, 84), administration on his estate to Phebe Schellinx, July 8, 1719.

ANNANIAS CONKLING (Lib. 11, 36), administration on his estate to his son Joseph Conkling, Oct. 22, 1730.

WILLIAM SCHELLUNX (Lib. 13, 371), yeoman, administration on his estate to William Schellunx, Apr. 19, 1740.

NATHANIEL BISHOP (filed but not recorded), will of May 1, 1685, in health and good mind, wife (not named), son Daniel, six and one half acres in Indian Well Plain to son Nathaniel; dau. Mary; Capt. Josiah Hobart and Samuel Mulford ex'rs.

In an ancient volume, known as "Sessions No. 1," in the office of the County Clerk of Suffolk, the following Easthampton wills occur.

WILLIAM HEDGES (p. 40), will of March 17, 1674, eldest son Stephen, wife Rose, son Isaac, four daughters (not named); wife ex'x; pro. Nov. 11, 1679; inventory appraised Sep. 29, 1674.

RICHARD STRATTON, Sr. (p. 57), will of Apr. 7, 1674, eldest son Richard, second son Thomas, wife Elizabeth, younger sons Isaac and Benjamin, dau. Elizabeth; wife ex'x; father in law William Edwards and bro. John Stretton, Sr., overseers; pro. June 7, 1676.

EDMUND SHAW, Sr. (p. 66), will of May 3, 1675, sons Thomas and Richard; two daus.; wives of Henry Ludlam and John Foster; pro. June 6, 1676.

JOSHUA GARLICK, Jr. (p. 78), will of Aug. 24, 1677, sons Joshua (under 21) and John, dau. Hannah and wife Elizabeth; capt. Talmage and John Mulford overseers; pro. Mar. 16, 1678.

WILLIAM FITHIAN (p. 113), will of Dec. 11, 1678, wife Margaret, who is ex'x; eldest son Enoch, son Samuel, daus. Sarah and Hannah; child of dec'd dau. Martha; son Samuel ex'r if he survives his mother, if not, then Enoch; Thomas Baker and Thomas James overseers; pro. Mar. 2, 1681.

THOMAS DIAMENT (or Dyment) disposed of his estate by making four deeds, of gift, which the Court of Sessions, sitting at Southampton on 7th, 8th and 9th days of March 1683, accepted as his will. The first, dated Aug. 21, 1677, recites a proposed marriage between his son James and Hannah, dau. of minister James, and the grantor binds himself to the minister to convey certain lands to the son to be enjoyed by him after the death of the grantor and his wife. The second, dated Dec. 27, 1680, gives to same son furniture and personal property. The third, dated July 28, 1682, recites the death of youngest son John, and gives James additional real estate, charging him and grantor's wife Mary to pay small legacies to daus. Sarah Headly of New Jersey, Abygayle, Hannah Bird, Ruth Dayton and Elizabeth Miller. The fourth instrument, also dated July 28, 1682, calls the grantor Thomas Dyment, Sr., and recites that having given the house and land at Georgica to his youngest son Thomas at his marriage, this is to convey to him other lands to take effect at the death of grantor and wife. (Dyment died, and a dispute about the division of his estate was settled Mar. 9, 1683 by agreement signed by the widow, minister James and Edward Howell, as recorded in same volume, p. 132.)

RICHARD SHAW, Sr. (p. 141), will of Sept. 7, 1680, wife Remember, five sons now at home, eldest Richard, second Edward, and William, Joshua and Benjamin; dau. Elizabeth under 18; son John has been given to grandparents Garlick; son Richard ex'r; pro. June 1683.

WILLIAM EDWARDS (p. 175), will of Feb. 1, 1681, sons John and Thomas; gr. son William, son of Thomas; gr. son, Josiah, son of John; dau. Sarah; gr. sons William, son of John, and Ephraim, son of Thomas; dau. Elizabeth Baker, dau. Ann Squire; five children of dau. Elizabeth, viz. Richard, Thomas, Isaac, Benjamin and Elizabeth Stratton; wife Ann ex'x; pro. Oct. 22, 1685; inventory taken Aug. 19, 1685.

JOHN PARSONS (p. 202), will of Mar. 5, 1686, eldest son Samuel under 21, sons John and Robert, brother Samuel Parsons; wife and daus. but not named; no ex'r named; pro. Mar. 16, 1686.

JOHN STRATTON, Sr. (p. 220), will of Aug. 30, 1684, eldest son John, second son Joseph, third Stephen, fourth Cornelius; gr. ch. Joseph, son of Stephen Hand; dau. Abigail, wife of Harry Norris; dau. Rebecca Busnell; dau. Ruth White; son Joseph; grandsons Steven Hand and Stephen Hedges; sons John, Stephen and Cornelius ex'rs; pro. Mar. 16, 1686.

JOHN MULFORD, Sr. (p. 230), will of Dec. 4, 1683, wife Freezneed, son John, eldest son Samuel; dau. Hannah, wife of Benjamin Conkline, who has five children; youngest dau. Mary, wife of Jeremy Miller, who has two children; bro. William Mulford; son John ex'r. Thomas James and bro. William overseers; pro. Oct. 19, 1686.*

WILLIAM MULFORD, Sr. (p. 238), will of Feby, 26, 1679, wife Sarah, eldest son Thomas (unmarried), sons William and Benjamin; two eldest daus. Sarah and Rachell, both married; wife ex'x; Samuel Mulford and Stephen Hedges overseers; codicil of Nov. 26, 1684; pro. Mar. 15, 1687.

BAZALLIELL OSBORNE (p. 243) uncupative will Feb, 11, 1687, bro. Jonathan, wife Elizabeth; bro. in law Arthur Howell and his two sons and dau. Elizabeth; bro. Joseph; proved on oaths of Benjamin Conkling, John Greenfield and John Enorrs; pro. March 17, 1687.

Recorded in the "Lester Will Book" in the office of the County Clerk of Suffolk are the following wills, etc.

* There is a bequest to "hester," and 5 sh. each to her three children, but nothing to indicate her relation to testator. Presumably she was a daughter, as the bequests to her children are the same as to his grandchildren.

THOMAS TALMAGE (p. 26), will of Apr. 23, 1687, wife Elizabeth, sons Nathaniel, Shubael and Onesimus; gr. son Thomas, son of Nathaniel; daus. Naomi, Hannah and Sarah Bee; sons Nathaniel and Onesimus ex'rs; pro. Sep. 29, 1691.

JOHN CARYLL (p. 42), letters of administration on his estate to Remember, his widow, Oct. 21, 1691.

STEVEN HAND, Sr. (p. 76), will of May 17, 1688, oldest son Stephen, sons Samuel and Joseph, and five daus.; wife Rebecca; letters of administration to widow, Apr. 15, 1693.

JOHN EDWARDS (p. 86), will of Aug. 25, 1685, wife Mary, oldest son Thomas, sons John, William and Josiah; wife ex'x; pro. Nov. 10, 1693.

THOMAS JAMES (Rev.) (p. 123), will of June 5, 1696, eldest dau. Sarah, wife of Peregrine Stanborough; dau. Mary, wife of John Stretton; dau. Hannah, wife of James Dyment; dau. Ruth, wife of Thomas Harris; gr. ch. Mary Stanborough and Mary Stretton; dau. in law Anne, now wife of Mr. Abraham Howell of Southampton, formerly wife of testator's son Nathaniel; eldest gr. son John M. Stanborough; dau. in law Mary, wife of John Mulford; dau. in law Elizabeth, wife of Joseph Osborn; sons in law Stanborough, Stretton, Dyment and Harris, ex'rs; sons in law Mulford and Osborn overseers; proved June 23, 1696.

Recorded in Liber A of Deeds in the Office of the County Clerk of Suffolk.

THOMAS CHATFIELD (p. 4), will of June 22, 1686, oldest son Thomas, wife (not named), dau. Anne, wife of Josiah Stanborough, dau. Elizabeth, wife of Edward Joanes, daus. Sarah and Mary, and son John; son Thomas ex'r, John Mulford Jr., Benjamin Osborne, and Thomas James, overseers; pro. Oct. 20, 1687.

JOHN OSBORNE (p. 7), dec'd May 2, 1687; inventory presented to Court of Sessions Oct. 19, 1687.

EASTHAMPTON.—WAINSCOTT,

THIS burying ground is in the southwesterly part of the township, at Wainscott, two thirds of a mile from the ocean, and a little more than that south of the main road between Easthampton and Bridgehampton. Most of the stones are of brown-stone, a few are of imported slate. This transcript is of all epitaphs antedating 1800 that were found there in Sept., 1887.

In Memory of
REUBEN EDWARDS
who died
Oct' 29th 1799,
in the 28th year
of his age.

In
Memory of
Lucretia, Wife of
Stephen Edwards,
who died
August 12, 1800,
in the 55 year
of her age.

In Memory of
NANCY
Daughter of
*Elifha & Mary
Conkling*
who died
March 15th 1797
*aged 2 years
and 3 days*

Nathan, Son of Elifha
& Elizabeth Conkling
deceaf'd Augt ye 16th
A.D. 1776 in ye 5th
Year of his Age

HERE lies the Body
of Ruth Ofborn
who died July ye 3^d
A.D. 1775. In ye 17th
Year of her Age.

HERE
LYETH THE
BODY OF M^r
IOSEPH STRAttON
WHO DEPARTED
THIS LIFE DECEMBER
THE 25 1722 AGED
72 YEARS AND
NINE MONTHS

In Memory
of Elifabeth
Daughter to
Mr James &
Mrs Mary
Hand Who
Died April
30 A.D. 1755
Aged 19 years

Jeremiah
Squier Died
July the 25th
1759 In ye 25th
year of his Age

Joanna Daughter of
Elifha & Elifabeth
Conkling died April
the 17th 1775 In ye 10th
Year of his Age.

In Memory of
Mr JOHN TALMAGE
who departed this life
Novr 2^d 1 7 6 4 ,
in the 86th Year
of his Age

HERE
LYETH · THE
BODY · OF
DANIEL · HAND
WHO · DEPARTED
THIS · LIFE
NOVEMBER · THE
17 · 1709 · AGED
20 · YEARS

In Memory of
James Hand Junr
who died Octo^r 2[0?]
A.D. 1757 in ye 52^d
Year of his Age
His Faith and practice
did Accord
Which prov'd he Lov'd
and fer'd the Lord
The path he trod fhin'd
as the Light
Of perfect Day which
ends the night.
Prov. IV. 18.

This Monument Erected
by Co^l Gardner, Capt
Mu^lford Lieu^t Dayton &
their Soldiers, is in
Memory of Jedediah
Ofborn, who was Kill'd
by the Discharge of his
Gun, Novr 30th 1772 in
the 21^{ft} Year of his Age.
How fudden was my Death
Life is but fleeting Breath

APPENDIX.

SOUTHOLD.—HASHAMOMACK.

A small burying-ground in Hashamomack, now Arshmomoque, a district lying between the villages of Southold and Greenport, east of Mill Creek, which runs almost across the Island. The creek was formerly known as Thomas Benedict's or Tom's Creek.

The deed for Hashamomack has not been found. The earliest conveyances in the Southold Town Records are those of James ffarrett, agent of the Earl of Sterling, to Matthew Sinderland, in 1639. Sinderland's widow married William Salmon who owned the Hashamomack land. Salmon's second wife, Sarah² Horton ¡(*Barnabas¹*), mar. 2d, Capt. John² Concklyne (*John¹*), whose descendants still own land at Arshmomoque. Henry Whitney, Edward Treadwell, Thomas Benedict and John Corey were early owners at Hashamomack.

The following inscriptions were copied in September, 1900, by Miss L. D. Akerly, and the accompanying notes have been prepared by her.

In Memory of
Mⁿ Ruth Wife
To Mʳ David
Corey died
Feb. 4 AD.
1739 in her 29 Year

In Memory of
Mⁿ Mary Relict of Mʳ
Grant Bradley
who died
May 5ᵗʰ 1785
in the 52ᵈ Year
of her Age.

In Memory
of John Conklin
died June yᵉ 16
1751
in yᵉ 64 year
of his Age

HERE LIES BURIED
THE BODY OF Mⁿ
SARAH CONKLING
WIFE OF Mʳ JOHN CONKLING
WHO DEPARTED THIS
LIFE AUGˢᵗ 17ᵗʰ
1753
AGED 89 YEARS.

In Memory
of Zerviah
the Wife of
William Rog-
ers who died
April the 22ᵈ 1775
Aged 67 Years

Abigail, Daughter
of Mʳ Nathaniel &
Mʳˢ Mary Tuthill
died Octʳ 26ᵗʰ 1769
Aged 6 years
Death is a debt to nature due
Which [illegible and partly buried.]

In Memory of
Mʳ Nathaniel Tuthill
Who died April yᵉ 8ᵗʰ
A.D. 1768, in yᵉ 37 Year
of his age

Our days are number'd we are told
Our life is but a Span
Ye living Mortals may behold
How frail a thing is Man.
His love to God & Faith was true
In Jesus who was Slain
Who will revive his Soul anew
At his return again.

Here lies
The body o[f Mʳˢ]
Susanna Conk [ling]
Wife of Mʳ
Samuel Conkling
Who departed this
Life Octʳ 8ᵗʰ 1753
in the 74ᵗʰ year
of her age.

Here Lies buried
the body of
Mʳˢ Temperance Conkling
Wife of Mʳ
Henry Conkling
Who departed this
Life Febʳʸ 25, 1739
In the 49ᵗʰ Year
of her age.

Here Lies Buried
The Body of
Henry Conkling
who departed this
life July 26ᵗʰ 1753
in the 63ᵈ year
of his age

Here lies the Body of
Mʳˢ Mary Conkling
the wife of Mʳ Joseph Conkling
who departed this Life
Auguſt the 16ᵗʰ 1752
in the 79ᵗʰ year
of her age

In Memory of
Lieut. Joseph Conkling
who departed this Life
Janʸ 20ᵗʰ A.D. 1739/40
in the 49 Year
of his age

In Memory of
Capt. Joſeph Conkling
of Southold, who departed this life
in the City of New York, the
25ᵗʰ of Dec. A.D. 1756
aged 29 years 1 month & 4 days.
Here's the juſt the generous & the Brave,
the Grave
Whoſe noble virtues ſtill ſurvive
Who paſt the Hardſhips dangers labour
toil
And now reſts quiet in his native ſoil.

RUTH COREY, d. 1739. David³ Corey (*Isaac,*² *John*¹), d. 1758,* mar. 1st, Mary Brush, 2d, RUTH Griffin, 22 Feb., 1722, who died 1739, and 3d, widow Mary Gillam.

MARY BRADLEY, d. 1785; her maiden name was Conkling; she was mar. Feb., 1754.

JOHN CONKLING, d. 1751, calls Henry Conkling his "brother" in his will on file in the N. Y. Surrogate's Office. He was son of John³ and Sarah.

SARAH CONKLING, d. 1753, aged 89, was not Sarah² Horton (*Barnabas*¹), who mar. Capt. John² Concklyne in 1657, but was doubtless wife of John³ Concklyne (Capt. *John*²). The will of Capt. John is given in Pelletreau's *Early Long Island Wills*;† that of his son John,³ before mentioned, is alluded to on p. 24 of this work, dated in 1705–6.

HENRY CONKLING, d. 1753, mar. Jan. 16, 1716–17, TEMPERANCE² Bailey (*Stephen*¹), b. Aug. 7, 1691, d. 1739. He mar. 2d, May 12, 1742, widow Mary Budd, dau. of Cartaret Gillam. She d. in 1771, wife of Silvanus Davis.‡ Henry's will is in N. Y. Surrogate, Lib. 18, 489.

Lieut. JOSEPH⁴ CONKLING, doubtless son of Joseph³ and Abigail (Tuthill) Conkling, grandson of Capt. John² Concklyne, b. Aug. 7, 1691, d. 1739-40, in his 49th year, His wife Lydia d. 1743.§ Their son, Capt. JOSEPH, d. 1756, mar. Sarah Wickham (*Joseph*).

NATHANIEL TUTHILL, d. 1768 (*Nathaniel,*⁵ *Daniel,*⁴ *John,*³ *Henry,*² *Henry*¹), mar. 1st, Michal Youngs,‖ 2d, Mary Havens. Their dau. ABIGAIL died 1769.

SUSANNA CONKLING (ward of Col. Isaac Arnold of Southold, who mar. her widowed mother) was dau. of John Washburn of Flushing and his wife Sarah (Cornell). Susanna mar. Samuel Conkling, doubtless son of Jacob² (*John*¹), in 1702.

* *Ante,* p. 18.
† See his epitaph, *ante,* p. 8.
‡ See her epitaph, *ante,* p. 18.
§ See her epitaph, *ante,* p. 14.
‖ See her epitaph, *ante,* p. 35.

INDEX I.

NAMES OF THOSE PERSONS WHOSE EPITAPHS ARE GIVEN IN THIS BOOK.

99

GOLDSMITH, GOOLDSMITH.

Bethiah, 1755, ... 4
Deborah, 1787, ... 3
Lydia, 1753, ... 4
Jeremiah, 1753, ... 5
John, 1724, 1779, ... 5
Zaccheus, 1706-7, ... 6
Zacheus, 1795, ... 3

GOOLDE.

Talmage, 1726, ... 65

GRANT.

Temperance, 1757, ... 66

GRIFFIN, GRIFFING.

Aaron, 1754, ... 13
Elisebeth, 1755, ... 13
Hannah, 1699, ... 13
Jasper, 1718, ... 15
Lydia, 1754, 1718, ... 13, 15
Parnal, 1764, ... 13
Robert, 1729, ... 14

HAINS.

Henry, 1796, ... 46
Sarah, 1796, ... 46

HALLIOCK, HALLUCK.

Bethiah, 1780, ... 6
Joseph, 1779, ... 6
Joshua, 1787, ... 6
Nathan, 1756, ... 12

HALSEY.

Mary, 1758, ... 19

HAND.

Daniel, 1709, ... 93
Elisabeth, 1755, ... 93
James, 1757, ... 93

HAUGHTON, see HORTON.

HAVENS.

Caleb, 1798, ... 43
Catharine, 1779, ... 44
Desire, 1771, ... 42
Easter, 1759, ... 44
Elmira, 1779, ... 42
Ezekiel, 1792, ... 41
Frances, 1763, ... 41
George, 1754, ... 45
Hannah, 1754, ... 43
Henrietta, 1784, ... 44
Jemima, 1772, ... 45
John, 1789, ... 45
Jonathan 1748, 1774, . . . 43
Jonathan Nicoll, 1799, . . . 44
Joseph, 1775, 1775, ... 45
Margaret, 1762, ... 44
Mary, 1768, ... 45
Nicoll, 1783, ... 44
Obadiah, 1786, 1787, . . . 43
Patience, 1762, ... 45
Phebe, 1752, ... 42
Ruth, 1759, ... 45
Sally B., 1801, ... 43
Sarah, 1767, 1767, 1790, . . 41, 44
Sidney, 1789, ... 42
Watson, 1785, ... 45
William, 1763, 1791, . . . 42, 43

HAZARD.

Elizabeth D. H., 1800, . . . 19

HEDGES.

Abiah, 1763, ... 70
D., 1769, ... 58
David, 1753, 1777, . . . 57, 58
Elias, 1755, ... 77
Elizabeth, 1772, ... 58

Hannah, 1792, ... 57
Jeremiah, 1742, 1738, . . . 71, 73
Jerusha, 1742, ... 73
John, 1778, 1786, 1742, . . 58, 58, 71
1737, 1759, 1759, . . . 71, 72
Josiah, 1767, 1769, ... 58
Lewis, 1738, ... 73
Lois, 1718, ... 75
Mary, 1768, 1712, ... 70, 71
Mehetabel, 1768, ... 75
Phebe, 1753, ... 58
Robert L., 1793, ... 57
Samuel, 1771, ... 58
Stephen, 1760, 17—, . . . 72, 73
Temperance, 1753, 1777, . . 57, 58
William, 1768, ... 70
William R., 1794, ... 60
Zerviah, 1792, ... 59

HEMPSTED.

Benjamin, 1772, ... 20
D., 1747, ... 20
Jerusha, 1792, ... 20
Kezia, 1756, ... 22
Mary, 1768, ... 20
Mehitabel, 1791, ... 22
R., 1746, ... 29

HOBART.

Mary, 1698, ... 16

HOPKINS.

John, 1727, ... 32
William, 1718, ... 32

HORTON, HAUGHTON.

Anna, 1781, 1753, 1783, . . 8, 9
Barnabas, 1787, 1680, . . . 8, 10
Bethia, 1722, ... 9
Bethiah, 1733, ... 12
Caleb, 1706, ... 9
David, 1772, ... 3
James, 1762, ... 9
Jonathan, 1707, 1768, . . . 10, 12
Lazarus, 1764, ... 7
Martha, 1793, ... 15
Mehetabel, 1773, 1787, 1772, 8, 8, 9
Patience, 1786, ... 9
William, 1788, ... 9

HOWELL.

Israel, N. H., 1800, . . . 24

HUBBARD.

Abigail, 1732-3, ... 5

HUDSON, HUTSON.

Elizabeth, 1738, ... 49
Jonathan, 1729, ... 49
Nathaniel, 1733, ... 49
Puah, 1762, ... 74
Samuel, 1738, ... 49

HUNTING, HUNTTING.

Clemence, 1776, ... 59
Edward, 1738, 1745, . . . 56
Elizabeth, 1719, ... 64
John, 1768, ... 59
Jonathan, 1750, 1771, . . . 55, 80
Joseph, 1711, 1738, . . . 64
Mary, 1706, 1745, 1733, . . 56, 64
1738, 1779, 1785, . . . 64, 80
Nathaniel, 1753, 1770, . . . 53, 80

HUTCHINSON, HUCHINSON.

Elijah, 1754, ... 17
Hannah, 1760, ... 17
Martha, 1717, ... 16
Mary, 1721-2, 1783, . . . 15, 17
Matthias, 1723-4, 1759, . . 16, 17
Phebe, 1784, ... 82
Samuel, 1717, 1737, 1790, . 16, 82
Thomas, 1748-9, ... 16

INDEX II.

NAMES OF ALL OTHER PERSONS.

84; Jonathan 84; Phebe 90; Rachel 84; William 84, 90; Zachariah 84.
SERLE, Joanah 86.
SHATTUCK, Samuel 48.
SHAW, Benjamin 91; Edmund 91; Edward 91; Elizabeth 91; John 84, 91; Joshua 91; Rebecca 84; Remember 91; Richard 84, 91; Thomas 91; William 91.
SHEFFIELD, Robert 30, 31, 34; Susannah 30, 31, 34.
SHERELL, SHERIEL, SHERRILL, Abraham, 90; Clemence 88; Jeremiah 76; John 39; Puah 75, 78, 86, 90; Recompense 39, 75, 79, 86, 90; Sarah 78; Stephen 90.
SINDERLAND, Matthew 94.
SMITH, Aylce 85; Nathaniel 62; Phebe Howell 62; Ruth 89.
SOLMON, Elizabeth 24; Hannah 24; John 24; Katherine 24; Mary 24; Rebecca 24; Sarah 24; William 24, 38.
SOUTHWICK, Cassandra 48; Lawrence 48.
SQUIRE, Ann 91.
STANBOROUGH, Anne 92; John M. 92; Josiah 92; Mary 92; Peregrine 92; Sarah 92.
STEER, Bithye 24; Elizabeth 24; Richard 24, 39.
STEVENS, STEEVENS, J. 78; Josiah 76.
STEVENSON, Marmaduke 48.
STIRLING, *Earl* 48, 94.
STODER, Elizabeth 39.
STORRS, John 15.
STRATTON, STRETTON, Abraham 87; Amy 88; Benjamin 88, 90, 91; Cornelius 91; David 87, 88; Eliphalet 56, 65, 87; Elizabeth 88, 90, 91; Hannah 88; Isaac 90, 91; Jeremiah 87; John 88, 90, 91, 92; Jonathan 71, 72; Joseph 84, 91; Mary 87, 92; Matthew 79, 88; Mehetable 71, 72, 88; Phebe 56, 65, 79, 87, 88; Rebecca 87; Richard 90, 91; Ruth 87; Samuel 42, 87, 88; Sarah 84; Stephen 88, 91; Thomas 90, 91; —— 85, 87.
STRONG, Martha 88.
SUNDERLAND, Matthew 24.
SYLVESTER, Brindley 46; Brinley 46, 48, 84; Elizabeth 33; Giles 48; Grizzell 84; Margaret 84; Mary 46; Nathaniel 33, 47, 48, 84; Patience 33, 47, 48.
SYMMES, Anna 34.

TABER, Amon 36; Sibbil 36.
TALMAGE, 91; Ann 88; Abraham 68; Catherine 78; Daniel 88; David 79, 88; Eanos 74; Elizabeth 92; Ennis 88; Enos 88; Hannah 92; Jeremiah 88, 89; John 88; Josiah 88; Mary 85, 86, 89; Naomi 92; Nathaniel 88, 92; Onessimus 66, 85, 92; Rachel 88; Rebeckah 85; Sarah 85, 87; Shubael 92; Thomas 86, 92.
TERRIL, TERRILL, Mary 84; Thomas 88.
TERRY, Abigail 38, 39; Daniel 38; David 39; Elizabeth 38; Esther 23; Gershom 38, 39; Hannah 39; John 38, 39; Jonathan 28, 33, 39; Lydia 28; Mary 39; Mehitable 39; Nathaniel 38; Patiance 33; Richard 38, 39; Robert 39; Ruth 38, 39; Samuel 38, 39; Sarah 39; Thomas 23, 33, 38, 39, 43.

THOMAS, Mary 89.
THOMSON, Isaac 90.
THORNE, Hannah 66; Joseph 66.
THORPS, Mary 87.
THROOP, Mercy 16; William 16.
TILLINGHAST, Joseph 77; Phebe 77.
TONGE, Anne 24; Elizabeth 24; John 24.
TOOKER, John 35. ⌐
TREADWELL, Edward 94.
TRENTE, Dorothy 85; Jonathan 85; Sarah 85.
TREVALE, Hannah 24.
TUTHILL, Abigail 96; Alethea 6, 9; Anne 6; Benjamin 23; Bethia 38; Daniel 8, 33, 35, 38, 40, 96; Dorothy 33; Elizabeth 35; Hannah 33, 34; Henry 30, 33, 34, 35, 38, 96; John 33, 35, 96; Jonathan 6, 9, 29, 33; Lydia 33; Mary 37, 95; Mehetable 8, 38; Michal 35; Nathaniel 35, 95, 96; Rufus 37.

USHER, Hezekiah 86.

VAIL, VAILL, Anna 39; Bethia 11; Eliza 29; Jeremiah 11, 29, 33, 39; John 39; Joyce 33; Peter 11; Thomas 39.

WALTERS, Robert 84.
WARNER, Nathaniel 39.
WARREN, Esther 33.
WASE, Anne 48.
WASHBURN, John 96; Sarah 96.
WEBB, Frances 27; Orange 27.
WELLS, Anna 6; Bethiah 39; Fregift 4, 6; Josha 24; Joshua 39; Mary 24; Thomas 6; William 6.
WHARTON, Edward 48.
WHEELER, Hannah 24; John 85; Joshua 24.
WHITE, Ebenezer 84; Elenor 87; Elnathan 87; Ruth 91.
WHITEHAIRE, Deliverance 24; William 24, 38.
WHITNEY, Henry 94.
WICKHAM, Abigail C. 23; Benjamin 39; Jacob 83; Jonathan 39; Joseph 39, 96; Lucretia 90; Marcy 60; Matthew 23; Samuel 39; Sarah 83, 96; Thomas 60, 89; William 39.
WIGGINS, John 6, 27, 32, 35; Mary 35; Thomas 27; William 27.
WINDES, Mary 38; Samuel 11.
WOODHULL, Elizabeth 15; Josiah 15.
WOODRUFF, WOODRUFFE, Abigail 85; Benjamin 45; Cattarina 85; Elizabeth 86; Mary 85; Seth 86.

YOUNGS, Anna 35; Benjamin 20, 21, 22, 40; Christopher 33, 35, 38; Daniel 24, 33; Dorothy 33; Elizabeth 33; Esther 33; Eunice 28, 35; Experience 39; Ezekiel 33; Gideon 28, 33, 35, 38; Hannah 26, 28, 38; Henry 33; J. 26; Jeremiah 33; John 4, 22, 24, 26, 33, 38, 40; Jonathan 28, 29, 33; Joseph 33, 35; Joshua 26, 33; Josiah 39; Marcy 21; Margaret 33; Mary 22, 38; Mercy 24; Michal 96; Phebe 29, 33; Rachel 35; Rhoda 26; Richard 29, 33; Sarah 33; Selah 22; Stephen 22; Susanna 33; Thomas 21, 22, 24, 26; Waite 40; Warren 33; Zerubbabel 26, 33.

www.ingramcontent.com/pod-product-compliance
Lightning Source LLC
Chambersburg PA
CBHW070928270326
41927CB00011B/2773